Workbook

Happily Ever After *Again*

Hope, Healing & Love For Second Marriages

SHARILEE SWAITY

Happily Ever After *Again* Workbook

A Companion Guide to Happily Ever After *Again*

Written and designed by

Sharilee Swaity

Grace Daily Publishing traverse Bay, MB 2020

ISBN 978-1-9990286-4-0

Published by Grace Daily Publishing
Traverse Bay, Canada.

Editing by Debra Butterfield and Paula Pietrobono
Cover Design by Sharilee Swaity
Interior Design by Sharilee Swaity

Please note that this book is designed to provide encouragement and motivation to its readers and is not intended to take the place of professional counselling services. It is sold with the understanding that the content is the sole expression and opinion of its author and should be balanced with the reader's good judgment.

The author shall not be liable for any physical, psychological, emotional, financial, or commercial damages, including, but not limited to, special, incidental, consequential or other damages. It is understood that the reader is responsible for their own choices, actions, and results.

If you are a group leader interested in purchasing a set of workbooks and/or books for your organization, please contact Sharilee Swaity at admin@secondmarriage.xyz, to enquire about a bulk discount.

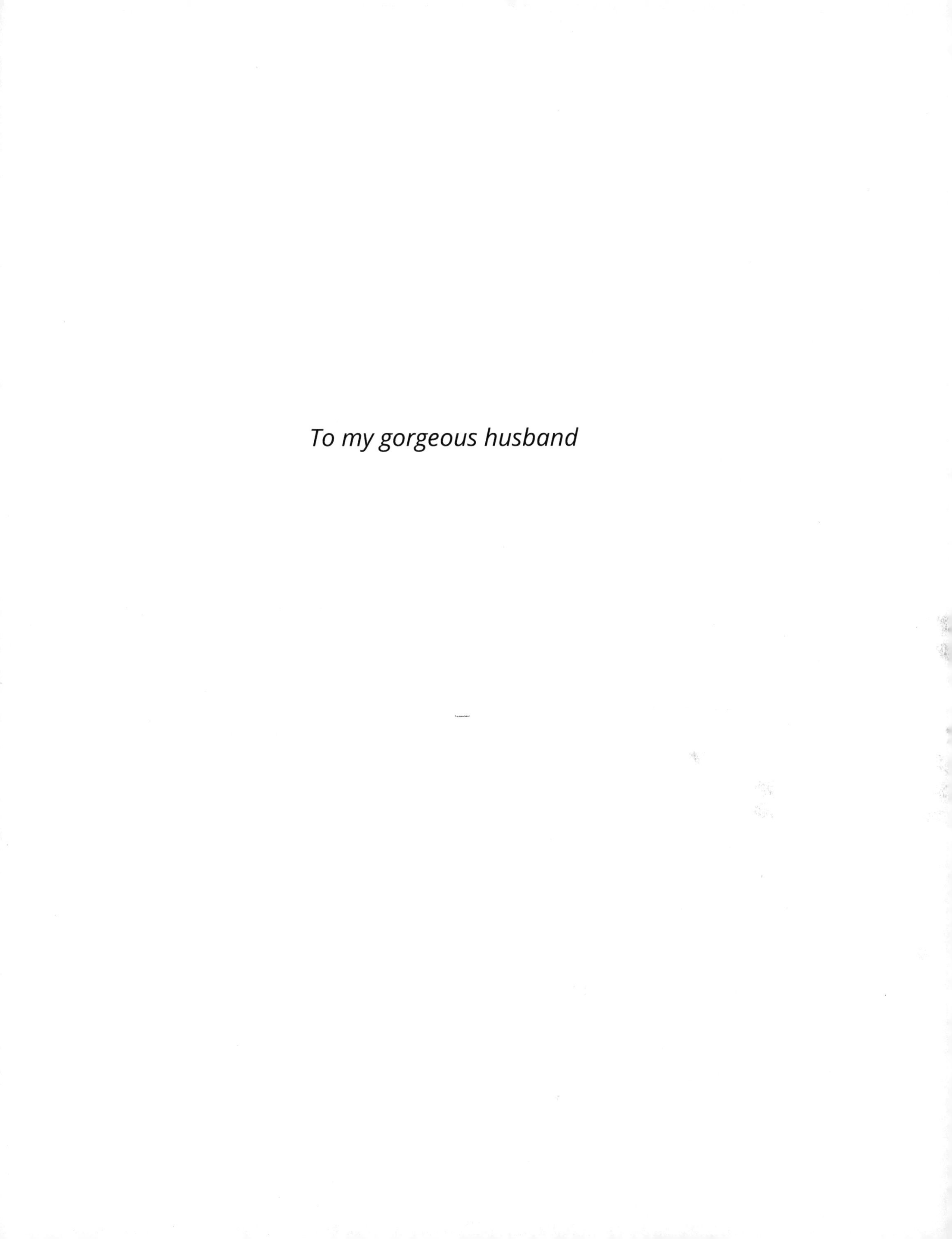

To my gorgeous husband

Table of Contents

Introduction

Are you in a marriage that seems far more difficult than you thought it would be? Are you looking for support for the unique challenges that a second (or third) marriage offers? If so, this workbook is made just for you. Whether you are experiencing undue stress from issues such as stepfamily conflict, insecurity, or trying to heal from the past, you will find specially tailored exercises and questions for couples with a history.

This book was inspired by the struggles that my husband and I faced at the beginning of *our* marriage. We came close to divorce, more than once. We fought endlessly and nasty things poured out of our lips. Instead of blessing and helping one another, we seemed to be destroying one another.

It took years of healing, learning and counselling to change our relationship. We both knew that we did not want our challenges to go to waste. It is for this reason that I started creating materials for those in difficult relationships. I hope this book is a blessing to you.

Let's face it. Second marriages are just different than first marriages. One (or both of us) have been through it all before. We are no longer as young. There are often other people, such as children and former partners, involved. Therefore, we may find that marriage advice for the never-married-before doesn't quite fit our situation.

Even if you or partner were not formally married but one or both of you were previously involved in a long-term cohabitation situation, the issues are very similar and this volume will apply to you.

This workbook is a companion guide to the book to *Happily Ever After Again: Hope, Healing & Love for Second Marriages,* and can be used alongside the book as a tool to help you get into the issues discussed in the book as they apply to your own life.

In this workbook, you will find helpful exercises and questions to expand on the concepts found in *Happily Ever After Again: Hope, Healing & Love For Second Marriages.*

Although I recommend that the two books be purchased together, this workbook will also stand completely on its own and may be used without the original book.

Please note that there is a free PDF workbook that goes along with the original book. This PDF is very useful as a free tool and can be printed off or used as a digital document.

It is available here: https://secondmarriage.xyz/sign-free-resources-page/

Many people, however, prefer a hands-on "real book," and this is for you. This print workbook is an expansion of the digital freebie and has over 100 pages of content not found in the free digital workbook, with plenty of room for writing down answers and exploring your feelings and thoughts about your marriage.

I encourage you to take as much time as you need to work through the exercises and reflection questions contained in this volume. This is your time to reflect on your marriage journey. No one needs to see what you are writing – it is your chance to be as honest as you can. Take advantage of it!

NOTE FOR COUPLES: This book can also be done by couples. If you are both working through the exercises, I would suggest that each member of the couple get their own book. Answering these questions and sharing your answers can help you gain valuable insights about one another and your marriage.

Some of the questions will apply more to the partner who was previously married and some to the partner of the person who was previously married. (If you are both, fill out both sets of questions.)

For Facilitators/Group Leaders/Counsellors

This workbook may be used in a group or marriage counselling setting. You may also wish to have the participants purchase the accompanying book, *Happily Ever After Again: Hope, Healing & Love for Second Marriages,* which gives more detail and background concerning the concepts taught in the workbook.

At the end of the book, I have included an appendix targeted specifically at facilitators and counsellors. Please look at this appendix for more detail about how to use this workbook in a group or counselling setting.

If you are a group leader interested in purchasing a set of workbooks and/or books for your organization, please contact Grace Daily Publishing at admin@secondmarriage.xyz, to enquire about a bulk discount.

Our Story

Twelve years ago, on a chilly spring day in late March, my husband and I got married. Our wedding was far from conventional. My wedding dress was an old prom gown repurposed from Value Village for under $30.

Our reception meal consisted of pulled beef, fry bread and salad served on plates held in our laps in my sister's living room. Afterwards, we had a cold marshmallow roast over the fire pit in her backyard.

It was casual and cozy, just like we wanted. It was also inexpensive; we desperately needed to save money for our actual married life. Another reason we decided to forego a traditional wedding was that it was a second marriage for both of us. We didn't feel comfortable having a big fuss about this union – we just wanted to be together.

Surprisingly, even though the wedding itself was unconventional, our journey to marriage was quite typical for couples entering remarriage. Like many marrying for the second time, we only dated a few months and were ill-prepared for the complications and issues that followed.

"WE DECIDED TO FOREGO A TRADITIONAL WEDDING BECAUSE IT WAS A SECOND MARRIAGE FOR BOTH OF US."

Introductory Assessment

The following assessment is designed to take a quick snapshot of your marriage. Please check off all the statements that are *true for you*. Just ignore any that are not applicable. **BE HONEST — NO ONE NEEDS TO READ THIS BUT YOU!**

PREMARRIAGE ISSUES

______ I am not sure if I was ready to marry.

______ I question why I even got married sometimes.

______ I can't figure out why our marriage is so hard.

DEALING WITH THE PAST

______ I feel sad that my ideal life didn't happen.

______ I don't know why I can't just "get over it."

______ I am not sure if I still need healing from the past.

______ I blame my former spouse for my divorce.

______ I haven't been able to forgive.

______ I sometimes feel insecure in my marriage.

______ I have a hard time learning to accept my story.

LOVING YOUR SPOUSE

______ It bothers me that our marriage lacks romance.

______ My spouse and I don't really know each other.

______ I wish my partner and I were better friends.

______ I wish we had better ways of handling conflict.

______ My partner and I have opposite personalities.

STEPFAMILY HELP

______ Our stepfamily is still adjusting.

______ Being a stepparent is hard for me.

TAKING CARE OF YOURSELF

______ I feel like I have lost myself in this situation.

______ I wish I had more support.

______ I think we might need marriage counselling.

Priorities Assessment

This next exercise will give you time to reflect on what parts of the book will be the most useful to you. Please number the following objectives from 1-10. 1 = Not at all important to you. 10 = Very important.

I WOULD LIKE TO:

_______ **Remember what drew me to marry my partner (Ch. 1 and 2)**

_______ **Understand why our situation sometimes feel so complicated (Ch. 3)**

_______ **Examine why my emotions seem so conflicted (Ch. 4)**

_______ **Deal with my disappointment about my current situation (Ch. 5)**

_______ **Understand why healing is so difficult (Ch. 6)**

_______ **Determine if I still need healing from the past (Ch. 7)**

_______ **Understand my own responsibility for failed past relationship(s) (Ch. 8)**

_______ **Learn to forgive (Ch. 9)**

_______ **Let go of insecurity in my marriage (Ch. 10)**

_______ **Accept "my own story," with all its imperfections (Ch. 11)**

_______ **Renew my belief in romance (Ch. 12)**

_______ **Get to know my spouse again (Ch. 13)**

_______ **Become better friends with my mate (Ch. 14)**

_______ **Learn to handle conflict better (Ch. 15)**

_______ **Deal with personality differences between my spouse and me (Ch. 16)**

_______ **Bond as a stepfamily (Ch. 17)**

_______ **Be encouraged as a stepmom (Ch. 18)**

_______ **To remember who I am as an individual (Ch. 19)**

_______ **To find outside support for my situation (Ch. 20)**

_______ **To decide if we should see a marriage counsellor (Ch. 21)**

How to Score the Priorities Assessment

Which of the preceding objectives did you rate the highest? List the top three below. *If there are more than three, simply choose the three that you feel are the most important to you. If there are less than three, choose your top ones.*

____

____

____

As you go through this workbook, these objectives will be your top goals for reading this book. Please write them down again in the area below. If you are the visual type, use markers or decorate them. *You may wish to go to these chapters first, especially if you are short on time.* At the end of the book, we will have a closing exercise to see if you have grown in these areas.

Top Three Goals

1. ______________________________

2. ______________________________

3. ______________________________

– 1 –
We Don't Want To Marry Again But...

After a marriage ends, either through divorce or bereavement, many people are understandably reluctant to marry again. The pain of losing someone they are so close to leaves many people unwilling to risk facing that loss again. In time, however, something changes the mind of the bereaved or divorced individual and gives them the confidence to walk down the aisle one more time.

The decision to marry someone who is divorced or widowed isn't an easy one, either. When you marry a previously married person, you know they come with extra baggage and a history that may affect your relationship. The following questions are designed to help you reflect on your decision to marry your partner.

FOR THE PREVIOUSLY MARRIED:

1. Think about your attitude towards marriage when you were first divorced or widowed. Immediately after losing your first spouse, which of the following statements best describes your feeling about getting remarried?

________ a. Never again!
________ b. Probably not
________ c. Maybe someday
________ d. I hope so
________ e. I am ready

2. If you answered *a*, *b*, or *c*, what were your reasons for not wanting to not marry again?

Example: You didn't want to go through another loss, you were unable to trust.

____

____

____

3. Do you think that any of the fears you used to have still affect your marriage today?

YES / NO / NOT SURE

4. If you answered yes above, how do you think these fears are still affecting you?

____

____

5. How long after your bereavement or divorce did you start to consider remarrying?

________ a. Ten years plus
________ b. 5-10 years
________ c. 1-5 years
________ d. Less than one year

6. If you were initially reluctant, what changed your mind about the possibility of walking down the aisle again?

___

___

___

7. How many years elapsed before you got married again?

a. Ten years plus
b. 5-10 years
c. 1-5 years
d. Under a year

THE PARTNER OF THE PREVIOUSLY MARRIED:

1. What was your reaction when your current spouse first brought up the idea of marriage?

a. Are you crazy?
b. Maybe in about ten years!
c. Possibly someday...
d. Sounds nice, but give it some time
d. Sounds great! Let's book the date!

2. If you were initially reluctant to marry your spouse, what was the reason? (Circle all that apply.)

a. Felt insecure about a previous partner
b. Felt like the person would have too much baggage
c. Felt uncomfortable dealing with stepchildren
d. Just didn't feel ready for that kind of commitment
e. Other:

____

3. If you changed your mind about marriage, what changed your mind and led you to go down the aisle?

____

____

— 2 —
You Got Married For A Reason

One third of divorced individuals get hitched within a year of signing divorce papers. A large number also choose to cohabitate soon after their marriage ends. In either case, commitment comes early and may later lead to regret or confusion. This can cause couples to wonder why they got married in the first place. This next exercise is designed to help you remember the reasons that you walked down the aisle.

HOPES AND DREAMS EXERCISE

Think back to when you were considering marrying your spouse. What were you hoping for? Write down as many reasons as you can think of. Be honest about your desires. Don't censor yourself out of embarrassment.

Some of your reasons may be more generic, such as "a partner to share life with." Other answers may be very specific, such as "someone who shares my love of soccer." Here are some questions to get you started.

- Were you hoping for a happy marriage?
- Were you hoping for a new family?
- Was sexual fulfillment a big priority for you?
- Were you hoping for a best friend?

Take some time to reflect on what your desires were before getting married. If you don't remember, ask the above questions and see if any resonate with you.

1. Make a list of the things you hoped for and desired when you married your spouse. (List as many as you can think of, whether or not they have been fulfilled or not, within the space provided.)

2. Out of the hopes and dreams you mentioned above, which ones are coming true in your marriage? (Even if not perfectly, at least to some degree.)

3. Which hopes and dreams have not been fulfilled yet?

Rediscovering the Why
For Your Marriage

4. Out of the reasons you wrote about in Question 1 above, which are the most important to you now, whether they are coming true or not?

1. ____

2. ____

3. ____

Even if your situation seems impossible right now, remember that you chose your partner and this family for a reason. There was something in your spouse you believed would be good for you. Below, reaffirm your commitment to work on your marriage and try to make your dreams come true.

I, ____________________, make a commitment on this day, ____________________ to continue to work on my marriage to ____________________.

Throughout this workbook, I will provide some space to draw things out. Use this space if you are more of a visual, creative person. If this does not match how you learn, feel free to ignore the drawing pages!

Below, draw out a picture of the things you dreamed about when you got married. Maybe you longed for romance, a happy family or a partner for board games. Draw out what you were looking for.

My Dream Letter Exercise

To finish off this chapter, you are going to write a letter to your spouse explaining your dreams for your marriage. Don't worry — you don't have to show them if you don't feel like it! The whole point is to get it on paper.

After you are done, you may wish to show your spouse, share it with your therapist, save it for yourself or throw it away. **Here are the instructions:**

1. Write the date.
2. Write a greeting (Dear [name of your spouse or favourite pet name])
3. Write about the things you were hoping for when you got married.
4. Tell her which of these have come true.
5. Tell him the most important things that you want now for your marriage.
6. Tell her how much you love her.
7. End with a closing.

Here is an example. Yours may be longer. Feel free to modify to suit your situation.

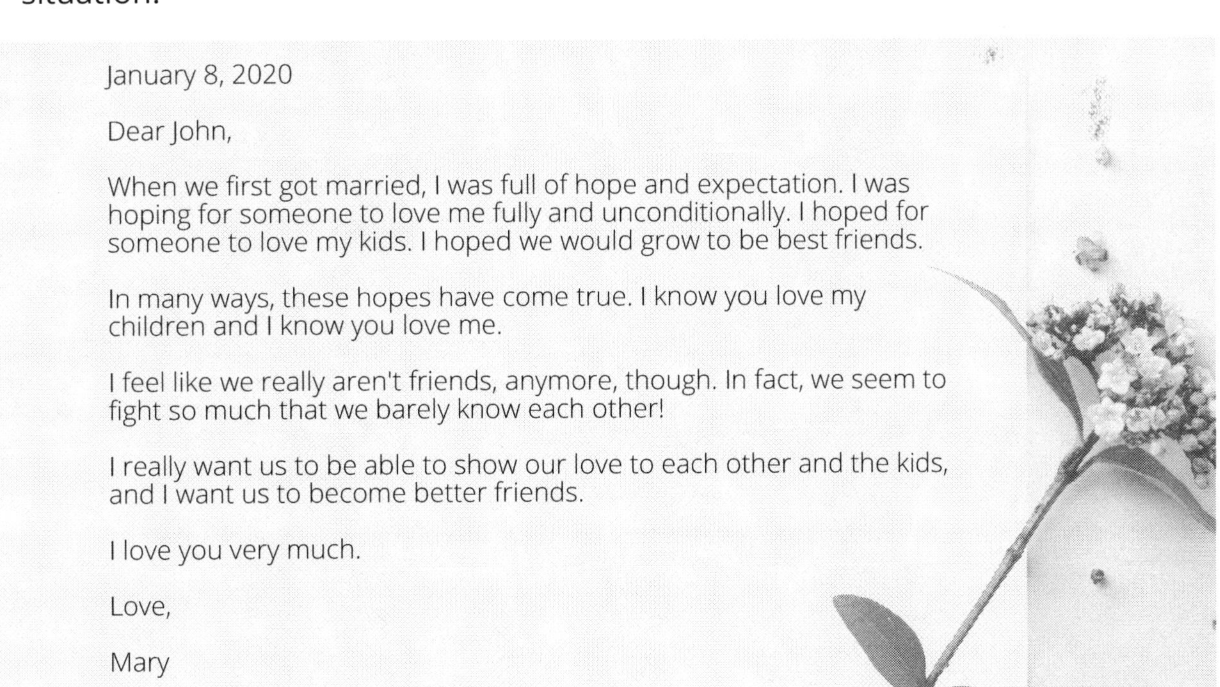

January 8, 2020

Dear John,

When we first got married, I was full of hope and expectation. I was hoping for someone to love me fully and unconditionally. I hoped for someone to love my kids. I hoped we would grow to be best friends.

In many ways, these hopes have come true. I know you love my children and I know you love me.

I feel like we really aren't friends, anymore, though. In fact, we seem to fight so much that we barely know each other!

I really want us to be able to show our love to each other and the kids, and I want us to become better friends.

I love you very much.

Love,

Mary

— 3 —
Why Are Things So Complicated?

A few years back, relationship statuses on Facebook were considered an important part of dating someone. When a couple started going out, they had to decide when to make their new relationship "Facebook official." Statuses on Facebook include married, engaged, dating or "it's complicated." This seldom-used Facebook relationship status means that an individual's relationship status can't be easily explained. (Such as dating an ex-partner while seeing new people?) Those of us in second marriages have complicated relationships, too. Our families are complex for many reasons.

This chapter will examine the factors that make a remarriage more complex than a first one. One way that a second marriage is more complicated is that there is always another spouse in the picture, whether in the past or in the present. The following quiz will help you determine how much of a factor an ex-spouse might be in your relationship.

1. Which of the following answers are most true for your situation? Please note that for some questions, these are options here for the person who was formerly married and the *spouse* of someone who was previously married. If you are both, feel free to answer for both.

________ a. I have a good relationship with my ex-partner(s). There are no children or the children are grown, so there is no need for frequent contact.
________ a. My first husband or wife passed away a long time ago and I have healed from this.
________ a. I know my spouse was previously married or widowed but it really doesn't cross my mind because it was long ago and doesn't affect us now.

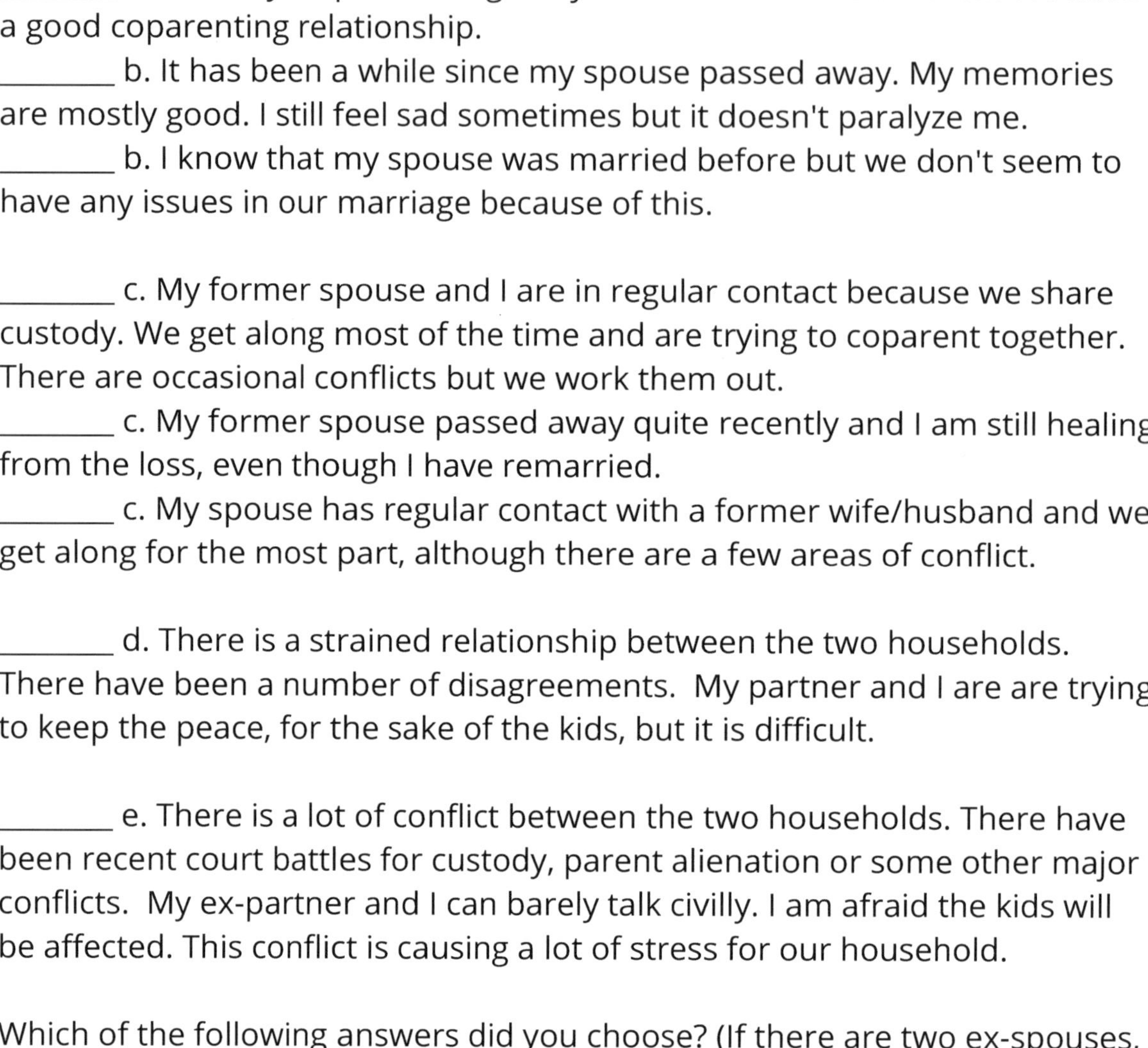

________ b. I see my ex-partner regularly because we share children. We have a good coparenting relationship.
________ b. It has been a while since my spouse passed away. My memories are mostly good. I still feel sad sometimes but it doesn't paralyze me.
________ b. I know that my spouse was married before but we don't seem to have any issues in our marriage because of this.

________ c. My former spouse and I are in regular contact because we share custody. We get along most of the time and are trying to coparent together. There are occasional conflicts but we work them out.
________ c. My former spouse passed away quite recently and I am still healing from the loss, even though I have remarried.
________ c. My spouse has regular contact with a former wife/husband and we get along for the most part, although there are a few areas of conflict.

________ d. There is a strained relationship between the two households. There have been a number of disagreements. My partner and I are are trying to keep the peace, for the sake of the kids, but it is difficult.

________ e. There is a lot of conflict between the two households. There have been recent court battles for custody, parent alienation or some other major conflicts. My ex-partner and I can barely talk civilly. I am afraid the kids will be affected. This conflict is causing a lot of stress for our household.

Which of the following answers did you choose? (If there are two ex-spouses, feel free to choose two answers.) Put a check mark beside whatever answer you chose. This shows the amount of influence your ex-partner is having on your household.

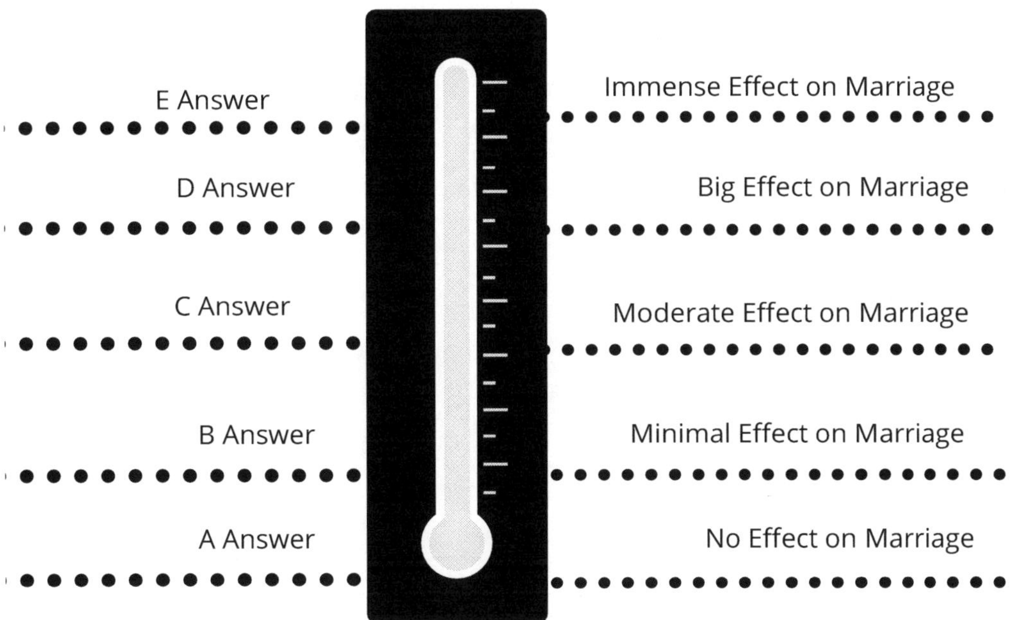
E Answer
D Answer
C Answer
B Answer
A Answer
Immense Effect on Marriage
Big Effect on Marriage
Moderate Effect on Marriage
Minimal Effect on Marriage
No Effect on Marriage

Complicating Factors Checklist

Besides the presence of ex-partners, there are several other situational factors that can create an extra layer of complications for second (or third) marriages. See which of the following factors apply to your circumstances.

The purpose of this exercise is simply to identify the level of complexity in your situation. In the next chapter, we will deal with the complicated emotions that can be present in a second marriage.

1. Check all that apply:

________ a. Shared or joint custody with one other household (1 point)

________ b. Shared or joint custody with two other households (2 points)

________ c.Stepbrothers and sisters (3 points)

________ d. Sibling rivalry between biological siblings (1 point)

________ e. Sibling rivalry between step-siblings (2 points)

________ f.Recent legal dispute (3 points)

_______ g. Mild case of parent alienation (2 points)

________ h. Severe case of parent alienation (3 points)

________ i. Rude behaviour from one person in family (1 point)

________ j. Rude behaviour from more than one person in family (3 points)

_______ k. Disagreement about disciplining the children (2 points)

_______ l. Financial difficulties (2 points)

_______ m. Recent household move(s) (2 points)

_______ n. Recent change of schools (2 points)

_______ o. Recent changes in household rules/routines (2 points)

Now, add up all your points. How many points do you have in total?

1-3 points: Mildly complicated
4-10 points: Pretty complicated
11-18 points: Very complicated
19-27 points: Majorly complicated

Were you surprised at how complicated your life was? Describe your feelings and thoughts about the complication level in your life.

____

____

____

____

The more complicating factors, the more likely it is that you and your partner will feel stress. Stress makes you more at risk for marital conflicts. If you are feeling the complications, so are your children.

1. Out of the list of possible factors complicating your marriage, which has been the most challenging for you?

____

2. How does this factor affect you?

____

____

3. How does this factor make you feel?

____

____

4. Out of the list of possible factors complicating your marriage, which do you think has been the most difficult for your spouse?

____

5. How has this factor affected your spouse?

____

____

6. How do you think this factor may be affecting your spouse emotionally?

____

In this space, if you are a visual learner, I want you to draw out the complications of your life.

— 4 —
Complicated Emotions

Circumstances are not the only way that remarriage tends to be more complex. The complexity also comes from inside, from our emotions. It is easy to assume that mixed emotions are a sign that your marriage is not working, but please be assured that these conflicted feelings are normal.

This chapter will list some common emotions that those involved in a second marriage may feel. We are not going to try to tackle these emotions yet but acknowledge them and become aware that they are there.

Following is a list of emotions you may be feeling. Don't be afraid to admit you are experiencing these. Admitting where we are emotionally is the first step to healing.

As you read each one, decide if this emotion is something you experience at times. Later on in the workbook, we will examine some tools for working through many of these emotions.

PLEASE NOTE: Some of these will apply to the partner who was previously married and some will apply to the partner who is *married* to someone who was previously married.

Complicated Emotions Checklist

1. For the following exercise, please write Y for YES, N for NO, NS for Not Sure, or NA for Not Applicable. After each emotion, I have included a short explanation.

________ a. JADEDNESS/CYNICISM
This is the feeling that you have been through this before, and that nothing will be that great again.

________ b. INSECURITY
This feeling can come from being cheated on, or from wondering about your partner's former's relationships. It can come from feeling like you aren't good enough for someone to love.

________ c. DEFEAT
This is the feeling that there is no point in trying because things probably won't work out anyway.

________ d. GUILT
This emotion can come from feeling like you are the one to blame, even if it is not logical, for the end of your marriage and for the suffering of your children. It can also happen to stepparents who wonder if they should have got married.

________ e. SADNESS/GRIEF
Because of the losses from divorce, bereavement and becoming a stepfamily, there can be sadness and grief.

________ f. ANGER
Anger can come up in us because of the difficulties that we have endured. It also can come from the difficulties in adjusting to marriage and from potential relationship issues with the former partner.

______ g. LONELINESS
Loneliness can come from family members feeling like strangers to each other.

Out of this list of emotions, which has been the most challenging for you personally (if any)? What makes it so challenging?

____

____

Out of this list of emotions, which do you think has been the most challenging for your spouse (if any)? What do you think makes it so challenging?

____

____

Just in general, how do you feel about your marriage situation right at this moment. Write freely.

____

____

____

____

____

____

—5—
Getting A New Perspective

In our culture, many of us anticipate our wedding date with great expectation. We are often brought up to believe that weddings are magical and that marriage will be our "happily ever after."

None of our childhood fantasies ever involved being married a second time. If we dreamt of marriage, it was of having our own children, with just one spouse forever after, and growing old together.

Being in a second marriage shatters those idealistic dreams. Our "forever after" wasn't forever and now we must deal with a new reality.

Part of healing is to learn to look at things differently. Look at what you do have instead of what you don't have. For example, look at how wonderful your husband is instead of what he isn't. Be grateful.

Being thankful for what you have may sound simplistic, but it is truly profound. When we learn to accept reality, it doesn't make it all better. We may still feel sad sometimes about the disappointments of our life. But thankfulness is a little seed that resides in our heart amidst the hurt, a promise of hope again and of a new life.

If you are the partner of a previously coupled person, you did not dream of being a stepmother and all of the pain involved in that role, either. You did not look forward to being the "second wife or husband" but that is the reality.

"I Sometimes Feel Bad" Exercise

Do this exercise if you are struggling with the fact that a second marriage is not what you had planned – not your ideal.

1. Write down 2-3 things that bother you about your family situation and that are hard to accept. Choose things that you don't have control over and cannot change. Start the statement with "I sometimes feel bad" ... or "I regret" or simply "I feel bad"

Here are some examples:

- I sometimes feel bad that my first marriage didn't last.
- I feel bad that my stepchildren don't seem to like me.
- I sometimes feel bad that I made unhealthy romantic choices.
- I regret getting married too soon because I wasn't ready.

Then write down the word, BUT, in capital letters, after each statement.

Now, after each statement, write down something good that contrasts with the statement that bothers you. I will show you some examples, based on our examples from part 1:

- I sometimes feel bad that my first marriage didn't last, BUT I am glad I met my second wife.
- I feel bad that my stepchildren don't like me, BUT I am grateful that they are close to their mom and dad. I believe they will come to trust me in time.
- I sometimes feel bad that I made unhealthy romantic choices, BUT I am grateful that I am learning good relationship skills now.
- I regret getting married too soon, BUT I am glad I am healing now and becoming whole.

STATEMENT #1

____

____ **BUT**

____

____

____

STATEMENT #2

____

____ **BUT**

____

____

STATEMENT #3

____

____ **BUT**

____

____

— 6 —

Why Is It So Hard to Let Go?

No matter how much we may try to deny it, it is important to remember that a second marriage is almost always born out of a great loss. In the case of a widower, someone has lost their life partner from this earth. The person whose relationship ended due to divorce or break up has lost a relationship they believed would endure.

This next exercise will examine the reasons that it is so difficult to heal from our past, despite our best intentions. If you would like to explore these topics in more depth, pick up a copy of the accompanying book, *Happily Ever After Again: Hope, Healing & Love for Second Marriages.*

"Reasons Healing is Difficult" Quiz

Answer the following questions with Y for YES, N for No, NS for NOT SURE and NA for NOT APPLICABLE.

1. Did you experience trauma in your childhood? ___________

2. Do you feel like you are doomed to having relationships never work out? ___________

3. Did you experience any of the following in your childhood: parents divorcing, parents constantly arguing, witnessing of abuse, being abused, severe bullying? ___________

If you answered yes to any of these, you may still need healing from incidents from your childhood. The more "yes" answers you gave, the more likely it is that you need healing from your early life.

4. Are you in regular contact with your ex-partner? ____________

5. Does your ex-partner regularly behave in ways that provoke conflict? ____________

6. Do you feel like you are not able to forgive your ex-spouse for their behaviour towards you? ____________

If you answered yes to any of these questions, the continued presence of your ex-partner is likely making it difficult for you to heal. The more "yes" answers you have in this section, the more likely it is that this issue is a problem for you.

7. When you lost your first spouse to death or divorce, did you feel pressure to "be strong" and not allow yourself to be overcome with grief?____________

8. Were you so busy trying to take care of your responsibilities when your first marriage ended that you did not have time to grieve? ____________

9. Did you suppress feelings of sadness, anger and disbelief after your marriage was over? ___________

If you answered yes to any of these questions, you may be still grieving from the loss of your previous spouse, whether through divorce or bereavement. The more "yes" answers you have in this section, the more likely it is that you are still grieving on some level.

10. When you went through your divorce or the death of your spouse, did you feel afraid or a sense of danger? ____________

11. Do you keep replaying things from the past over and over again?

____

12. After the loss of your spouse, did you experience any of the following symptoms: racing thoughts, flashbacks, anxiety, insomnia? ____________

If you answered "yes" to any of the preceding questions, it is possible you may have had a trauma-based reaction. If you suspect you may still be experiencing a trauma-based reaction, consider talking to a professional (psychologist, counsellor or a doctor) who can help you work through these issues.

— 7 —

You Might Still Need Healing If...

How can you tell if you still need healing from the past? This chapter has a list of clues to look for. Read through this list and check off each one that applies to you. Be honest with yourself — no one else needs to read this.

______ You Lack Trust

One of the most common signs that we still hurt is distrust. When someone in our past does something to break our trust, we have trouble trusting our present partner. Are you having trouble trusting your current partner even though they deserve your trust?

______ You Are Jealous

If you are jealous and insecure about your relationship, this is a strong sign that you are still being affected by your past. Unless your spouse has given you good reason to doubt them, consider that you are likely reacting out of fear from past rejection and betrayal. Do you struggle with jealousy and insecurity with your partner for no good reason?

______You Are Bitter

Feeling bitter can be another sign that your past is still strongly influencing your present. Bitterness makes us feel cynical with an edge of anger towards others, unable to get too close or hope for something good. Do you sometimes find yourself becoming angry for no apparent reason?

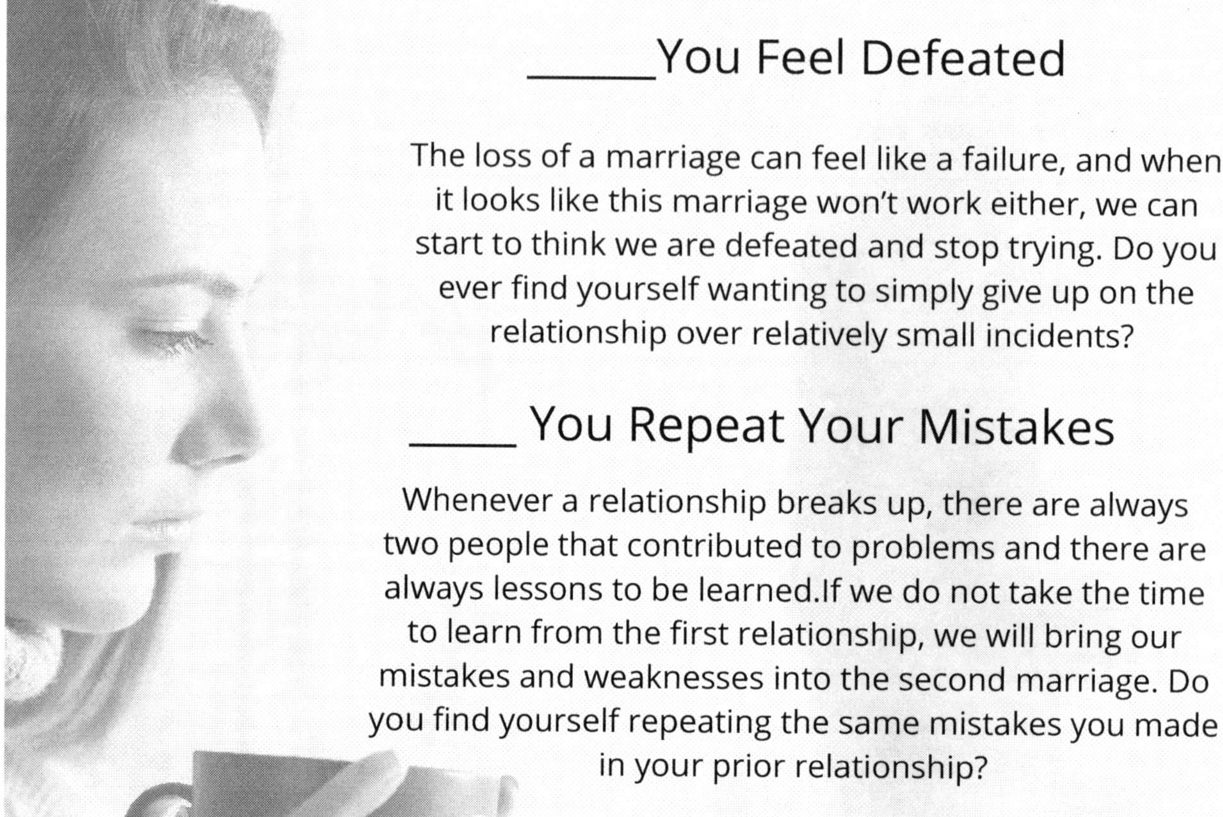

______You Feel Defeated

The loss of a marriage can feel like a failure, and when it looks like this marriage won't work either, we can start to think we are defeated and stop trying. Do you ever find yourself wanting to simply give up on the relationship over relatively small incidents?

_____ You Repeat Your Mistakes

Whenever a relationship breaks up, there are always two people that contributed to problems and there are always lessons to be learned.If we do not take the time to learn from the first relationship, we will bring our mistakes and weaknesses into the second marriage. Do you find yourself repeating the same mistakes you made in your prior relationship?

1. On a scale of 1-10, how much do you believe that you have let go of what happened in previous relationships? (1 = I haven't let go of the past at all, 10 = The past is completely irrelevant to me.)

1 2 3 4 5 6 7 8 9 10

2. Using the samescale of 1-10, how much do you believe that your spouse has let go of the past?

1 2 3 4 5 6 7 8 9 10

3. Which of the following signs, if any, does your spouse exhibit in their life?

________ a. They find it difficult to trust you.
________ b. They act jealous or insecure.
________ c. They display a sense of bitterness and quiet anger.
________ d. They seem defeated, believing this marriage will fail.
________ e. They seem to be repeating patterns from the past.

4. For any of the behaviours that apply to you or your spouse, write 1-2 sentences giving more detail about how this characteristic is showing up in your marriage.

a. Difficulty trusting:

____

____

____

b. Jealousy:

____

____

____

c. A sense of bitterness and quiet anger

____

____

____

d. Sense of defeat, and feeling as if your marriage is going to fail

____

____

____

e. The sense that you are repeating mistakes from your previous relationships

____

____

____

Do not be discouraged if you have some of the signs of not being healed. Acknowledging a problem is always the first step towards fixing it. Unless you are honest with yourself, you can't heal.

It is a good idea to get into regular disciplines which help you acknowledge your feelings, such as journaling and praying. Talking to a good counsellor can benefit greatly, too. Remember that healing is a process.

— 8 —
Take Ownership

The next step in letting go of the past is to take responsibility for your part in what happened so that you do not keep repeating the same old patterns. The next exercise is designed to help you take an honest look at your previous relationship(s) and how they may be connected to your present relationship.

"Digging Up Bones" Exercise

This exercise is designed to see how unhealthy patterns from your first marriage (or other relationships) may be continuing in your current marriage. Write down the answers to the following questions.

ISSUE #1

1. What was one of the main issues that you and your ex-partner fought about? Be as specific as possible. *Example: fighting over who does the housework.*

____

____

2. For this issue, what did your ex do that contributed to the problem? *Example: they always complained that the house wasn't clean enough but they never helped.*

____

____

____

3. What did you do that contributed to the problem? *Example: I always nagged and got angry with them.*

____

____

____

____

4. Is this issue a concern in your current marriage?

YES / NO

Answer the following questions if you answered YES to this issue being a problem in our current marriage.

5. How is your spouse contributing to the issue? *Example: My spouse doesn't do much around the house and it really irritates me!*

____

____

____

6. What are you doing that contributes to the problem? *Example: I nag them constantly and yell at them almost every day.*

____

____

____

7. Are you handling this issue in the same way you handled it before? How so? *Example: Yes, in both my marriages, I nagged my spouse about not doing things around the house.*

---

8. How could you handle this issue differently to get better results? *Example: I could be more proactive and draw up a schedule for housework and let my spouse choose which tasks to complete.*

ISSUE #2

1. What was another issue that you and your ex disagreed on? Be as specific as possible.

____

____

2. For this issue, what did your ex do that contributed to the problem?

____

____

____

3. What did you do that contributed to the problem?

____

____

____

4. Is this issue a concern in your current marriage?

YES / NO

If YES, answer the following questions.

5. How is your spouse contributing to the issue?

____

____

____

6. What are you doing that contributes to the problem?

____

____

____

7. Are you handling this issue in a different way than you handled it before? How so?

____

____

____

8. How could you have handled this issue differently to get better results?

____

____

____

____

– 9 –

Forgiveness

Forgiveness is the third step in healing but it is very difficult to do sometimes. When we can't forgive others, we risk becoming bitter and taking it out on those we love. Forgiveness frees us to begin each day afresh.

Even if you can't forgive someone now, try to make a resolution to at least try to forgive them sometime in the future. This next exercise will help you see who you may need to forgive.

Forgiveness Exercise

Here is a list of individuals you may find hard to forgive. Check each person(s) that you need to forgive in your life.

________ 1. Yourself

________ 2. Your ex-partner(s)

________ 3. Your parents or other people in your childhood

________ 4. Your spouse's ex-partner

________ 5. Your stepchildren

________ 6. God

________ 7. Other ________________________________

In the circles below, write down the names of the three people you find most difficult to forgive (if there are less than three, that's okay, of course.) Then, write what the person did to hurt you (summarize) and whether or not you are willing to try to forgive them sometime in the future.

Name:

____

How they hurt you (summarize it):

____

____

____

Are you willing to try to forgive?

____

Name:

____

How they hurt you (summarize it):

____

____

____

Are you willing to try to forgive?

____

Name:

____

How they hurt you (summarize it):

____

____

____

Are you willing to try to forgive?

____

The final step in healing from your past is to change your thoughts. Transformed thoughts lead to transformed feelings. When we have baggage from our past relationships and hurts, we may tend to see our present partner through the lens of the past. For example, if a woman's ex-husband cheated on her, she will tend to think that all men cheat and think that this husband is sure to be disloyal, too.

A powerful way to stop seeing your partner through the warped view of past hurts is to remind yourself of why you married your current partner in the first place. This next exercise is designed to do this.

"What I Love About You" Exercise

This exercise asks you to write down a list of eight things that you like about your spouse. You can be as specific or as general as you like. A specific example might be "I love how you smile at me in the mornings." A general example might be "I love how you are hard-working."

If you would like a printable version of this exercise, go to the following address to pick up your free printable:

https://secondmarriage.xyz/ten-things-i-love-about-you-download/

1. Fill in the following sentences, with your spouse's name on the top.

2. Now, photocopy (or print from address above) your list and put it somewhere where you can see it. If you start to judge your spouse through the filter of your past, remind yourself of the things that you like about your spouse. *This* is who he or she is, not the person from your past!

#1: I Love How You...

#2: I Love How You...

#3: I Love How You...

#4: I Love How You...

#5: I Love How You...

#6: I Love How You...

#7: I Love How You...

#8: I Love How You...

– 10 –
When You Feel Insecure

Do you ever feel insecure or jealous in your marriage? If so, this chapter is for you. Overcoming insecurity is one of the most challenging things to do, especially if you have been cheated on, lied to, abused or abandoned. It may take everything in you to learn to trust again. This chapter is to help you deal with the issue of insecurity in your marriage.

Reflection Questions

1. On a scale of 1-10, how insecure would you say you are in your marriage? (1 = Completely secure, 10 = Completely jealous and insecure)

1 2 3 4 5 6 7 8 9 10

Answer the following questions if you scored yourself as five or higher.

2. Has your spouse ever given you a reason to be insecure with his or her behaviour? YES / NO

3. If you answered YES, what has she or he done that led you to feeling insecure?

____

____

____

4. Has your spouse ever apologized for this type of behaviour? YES / NO

5. Do you think the insecurity is stemming from something in your past?

YES / NO / MAYBE

6. If yes, what events happened in your past that led to you feeling insecure?

____

____

____

7. If he/she has not done anything to elicit your distrust, can you make a decision to trust your spouse? YES / NO

8. If YES, please write down your commitment to trust your spouse below.

____

____

Remind yourself of your commitment when you start to act insecurely because of your past.

9. If NO, what would it take for you to trust your spouse? Write it down below.

____

____

____

10. On a scale of 1-10, how insecure would you say your spouse is regarding your marriage?

1 2 3 4 5 6 7 8 9 10

Answer the following questions if you scored your spouse as five or higher.

11. Have you ever given your spouse reason to be insecure with your behaviour? If so, what have you done?

____

____

____

12. Have you ever apologized for this behaviour? YES / NO

13. Do you think the insecurity is stemming from something in his/her past? YES / NO

14. If yes, what events happened in his/her past that led to him/her feeling insecure?

___

___

___

15. If you have not done anything to elicit your spouse's distrust, can you ask your spouse to decide to trust you? YES / N0

16. Write down what your spouse said when you asked him/her to trust you.

___

___

— 11 —
Accepting Your Story

When our marriage ends, we lose the dream of forever after and are forced to accept a different reality than the one we had imagined. Part of healing is learning to accept our story. A powerful way of doing this is to share our narrative with someone else. Writing our story out, even if we don't share it with anyone, is also a powerful way of healing.

DISCLAIMER: I would only recommend doing the exercise in this chapter if you feel you can talk about your past without getting too upset. If you are still raw and hurting, save this exercise for a later time.

"Tell Your Story" Exercise

In this chapter, you will find the same exercise done in two different ways. The first way is to share your story verbally with another person, using a set of questions. The second way is to write down the answers to the provided questions. After you have written the answers, you can either keep them to yourself or share it with someone else, whatever you feel comfortable with.

To avoid confusion, I will list each version of the exercise separately with its own instructions. Please choose which method of the exercise you feel more comfortable with. (You could do both if you like, too!)

Here are the two versions of the exercise:

"Speak Your Story" Exercise
"Write Your Story" Exercise

If you are not sure of which version of the exercise to try, here some things to consider.

- If you don't enjoy writing, do the oral version.
- If you want to save time, do the oral version.
- If you don't want a record of this for anyone to see, do the oral version.
- If you would like to keep a copy of your story to share with someone else, do the writing version.
- If you enjoy writing and find it helps you heal, do the writing version.

Which version of the exercise (if any) are you going to do? (Remember that this exercise is only for those who feel healed enough to talk or write about their story without being triggered.

__________ None

__________ "Speak Your Story" Exercise

__________ "Write Your Story" Exercise

__________ Both versions of the exercise

"Speak Your Story" Exercise

The following exercise is designed to help you tell your relationship story: all the parts, both good and bad. Please remember to only do this exercise if you feel like you can talk about it without getting upset.

To do this exercise, you need to find someone to help you with it. Ask someone (the interviewer) to read you the questions aloud, with you answering each one, in an interview style. Choose someone who is a good listener and is willing to take the time to finish this with you. It should take about 5-12 minutes.

DIRECTIONS

1. The interviewer reads out all the introductory text before each set of questions (in bold).

2. The interviewer reads each question and then gives you as much time as you want to answer the questions.

3. Answer each question as best as you can recall. Don't worry about being thorough but instead just try to keep moving through the questions.

4. Stick to the facts. Don't make judgements or focus on the emotions of it. Include both the negative and positive parts of your story. Aim for a balanced view.

5. Be sure to keep this private from your children if they are too little. Try to make sure you will have privacy when you are doing this exercise. This is something you could also do with a counsellor.

PART ONE: ANSWER THE FOLLOWING QUESTIONS REGARDING YOUR MOST SIGNIFICANT PREVIOUS RELATIONSHIP.

1. What was the name of your former partner?

2. How did the two of you meet?

3. How long did you date before marrying?

4. How old were you when you got married?

5. Did the two of you have children? What are their names?

6. What place(s) did you live during your marriage?

7. What did the two of you enjoy doing together?

8. How often did the two of you argue or have disagreements?

9. What were the arguments about?

10. How long were you married or together?

PART TWO: ANSWER THE FOLLOWING QUESTIONS IF THE RELATIONSHIP ENDED IN DIVORCE / BREAKUP.

11. What precipitated the breakup?

12. Who initiated the divorce/breakup?

13. Was there adultery, abuse or abandonment involved?

14. What was your emotional state for the first few months after the divorce/breakup?

ANSWER THE FOLLOWING QUESTIONS IF YOUR FORMER PARTNER PASSED AWAY

15. What was the cause of your spouse's passing?

16. Did you know your spouse was going to pass beforehand or was it a surprise?

17. If you knew, what was the time before her/his passing like?

18. What supports did you have to help through the first few months after their passing?

19. How do you honour your them in your life now, if at all?

PART THREE: ANSWER THE FOLLOWING QUESTIONS REGARDING YOUR TIME BETWEEN MARRIAGES/RELATIONSHIPS

20. How did you grow as a person during the time between your previous relationship and this current one?

21. Did you date anyone between relationships?

22. Did any of these dates lead to any serious relationships?

23. What were the main reasons that this/these relationship(s) did not work out?

Now, imagine a little cabinet in your mind with several drawers. One of the drawers is empty. Open it and place that story in the drawer.

If you are a believer, thank God for this part of your life. You learned from it, and it has made you into the person you are today. It is part of your history, but now you are placing it in its right place: the past. You are now working on an exciting new chapter in your life!

PART FOUR: ANSWER THE FOLLOWING QUESTIONS REGARDING YOUR CURRENT MARRIAGE

24. How did the two of you meet?

25. What was your first impression of your current partner?

26. How long did you date?

27. Did you ever break up before getting married? If yes, what caused the breakup? When did you get back together?

28. If either one of you has children, when did the children meet their future stepparent(s)? How was that meeting?

29. Where did you get married? Describe your wedding in one or two sentences.

30. How did it feel to tell your story in a neutral fashion?

"Write Your Story" Exercise

The following exercise is designed to help you tell your relationship story: all the parts, both good and bad. Please remember to do this exercise only if you feel like you can write about it without getting upset.

DIRECTIONS

1. Answer each question the best you can. If you don't remember, just keep moving.

2. Stick to the facts. Don't make judgments or focus on the emotions of it. Include both the negative and positive parts of your story. Aim for a balanced view.

3. Be sure to keep this private from your children if they are too little to know all the details. You might want to keep this to share with them when they are older.

4. You could also share this story with your counsellor or someone else, if you wish to.

5. If you enjoy writing and storytelling, you could take these questions and re-write this into a narrative and a story that flows.

PART ONE: ANSWER THE FOLLOWING QUESTIONS REGARDING YOUR MOST SIGNIFICANT PREVIOUS RELATIONSHIP

1. What was this person's name?

____

2. How did the two of you meet?

____

3. How long did you date before marrying?

____

4. How old were you when you got married?

____

5. Did the two of you have any children? If so, what are their names?

____

____

6. What places did you live during your marriage?

____

____

7. What did the two of you enjoy doing together?

____

8. How often did you have serious disagreements?

____

9. What were the arguments about?

____

____

10. How long were you married?

____

PART TWO: ANSWER THE FOLLOWING QUESTIONS IF YOUR MARRIAGE ENDED IN DIVORCE/ A BREAKUP

11. What precipitated the breakup?

____

____

12. Who initiated the breakup? ________________________

13. Was there abuse, adultery or abandonment involved?

____

____

14. What was your emotional state for the first few months after the relationship ended?

ANSWER THE FOLLOWING QUESTIONS IF YOUR FORMER PARTNER PASSED AWAY

15. What was the cause of your spouse's passing?

---

16. Did you know your spouse was going to pass beforehand or was it a surprise?

---

17. If you knew, what was the time before her/his passing like?

---

18. What supports did you have to help for the first few months after they passed away?

---

19. How do you honour them in your life now, if at all?

____

PART THREE: ANSWER THE FOLLOWING QUESTIONS REGARDING YOUR TIME BETWEEN RELATIONSHIPS

20. How did you grow as a person between your previous relationship and the current one?

____

____

21. Did you date anyone else in between your two main relationships?

YES / NO

22. Did any of these dates lead to any serious relationships?

YES / NO

23. If yes, what were the main reasons that this/these relationship(s) did not work out?

____

____

Once you have shared this part of your story, I want to you to imagine a little cabinet in your mind with several drawers. One of the drawers is empty. Open it and place that story in the drawer.

If you are a believer, thank God for this part of your life. You learned from it, and it has made you into the person you are today. It is part of your history, but now you are placing it in its right place: the past.You are now working on an exciting new chapter in your life!

PART FOUR: ANSWER THE FOLLOWING QUESTIONS REGARDING YOUR CURRENT MARRIAGE

24. How did the two of you meet?

____

25. What was your first impression of your current partner?

____

____

26. How long did you date?

____

27. Did you ever break up before getting married? If yes, what caused the breakup? When did you get back together?

____

____

____

28. If either one of you has children, when did the children meet their future stepparent(s)? How was that meeting?

____

____

29. Where did you get married? Describe your wedding in twenty words or less.

____

____

____

30. How did it feel to write your story in a neutral manner?

____

____

– 12 –

Are We Destined for Love?

Are you in love with your spouse? In love with that giddy excitement a couple feels when they first start dating? Do you feel passionate about your partner? Or do you believe that passion and romance are something reserved for the very young?

I think many of us long for more passion and romance in our marriage, even if we don't admit it. In a second marriage, though, it can be especially difficult to find and maintain a sense of connection because of the stresses and complications we face.

In this chapter, we are going to examine what research has to say on the topic of romance. Specifically, we will look at two studies out of Stony Brook University to give us clues for how couples can develop and maintain a sense of closeness. Then, in the next two chapters, we will learn specific strategies for implementing what we have learned.

The first study we will consider is a very interesting one called "Neural Correlates of Long-Term Romantic Love"[1] The title is kind of boring but the findings of the study are quite exciting!

[1] Bianca Acevedo, Arthur Aron, Helen E. Fisher, and Lucy L. Brown. 2012. "Neural correlates of long-term intense romantic love." Social, Cognitive and Affective Neuroscience 7 (2): 145-159. Accessed March 22, 2017. https://academic.oup.com/scan/article/7/2/145/1622197/Neural-correlates-of-long-term-intense-romantic#.

The researchers examined a group of older couples who had been married for a long time (most of them for over twenty-five years) and still considered themselves very much in love with their spouse.

First of all, they examined the brain activity of these couples and found that their physiological response to talking about their husband or wife was very similar to young couples who had just met. In other words, they still had the butterflies around their spouse! Isn't that amazing?

The scientists then looked for commonalities between the couples: clues for what made these relationships so special. What they found was that most of the couples who reported to be in love *after twenty-five years* had the following characteristics:

1. **They made love frequently**
2. **They had a strong emotional attachment**
3. **They were good friends**

KEYS TO ROMANCE

So, they were physically close, emotionally close and mentally close. Wow, that sounds good, doesn't it? It is encouraging to realize that the "in-love" feeling we see idealized in movies and romance novels is not necessarily separate from our actions.

The feeling of being in love corresponds with specific actions: making love, staying emotionally intimate and being friends. These are all things that we can work on.

Another intriguing study from the same university gives us more clues to finding emotional intimacy with our partner. It is called "The Experimental Generation of Interpersonal Closeness."[2]

This project, headed by husband and wife team Arthur and Elaine Aron, is absolutely fascinating. The professors paired students in their psychology classes and instructed the young people to ask each other a series of increasingly intimate questions. There were 36 questions in total, all designed to get to know each other better.

At the beginning and the end of the exercise, participants were tested on how close they felt to each other. After answering the 36 questions with one another, the pairs of students felt substantially closer to one another. Another very revealing part of the results of the study was that even people who were significantly opposed in values felt much closer after the study. This tells us that we can still feel close to someone that is very different from ourselves. Even if we are opposites, we can still feel close to our partner.

What is the key to feeling close to our spouse? The key to intimacy is sharing of ourselves. Ironically, when two people try to hide their true feelings from one another, in order to keep the peace, they are missing out on the one thing that could actually build that sense of closeness, in spite of the problems.

2. Arthur Aron, Edward Melinat, Elaine N. Aron, Robert Darrin Vallone Darrin and Renee J. Bator. 1997."The Experimental Generation of Interpersonal Closeness: A Procedure and Some Preliminary Findings." *Personal and Social Psychology Bulletin 23* (4): 363-377. Accessed March 22, 2017. http://journals.sagepub.com/doi/pdf/10.1177/0146167297234003.

Reflection Questions

1. Have you ever longed for more passion in your marriage? YES / NO

2. Think about a loving couple you know who have been together for a long time. This could be anyone, whether your parents or some friends from church. Write down two words that could describe their relationship, and give a brief explanation of how this trait shows up in their relationship.

Example:

Affectionate – They always hug and kiss one another when they are leaving to go somewhere.

Fun – They are always making jokes with each other.

Trait #1: ______________________________

How it shows up:

____

____

Trait #2: ____________________________________

How it shows up:

____

____

3. Which one of the following findings from the studies mentioned above did you find most interesting?

_______ a. Intimate conversations lead to closeness
_______ b. We can be opposites but still feel close
_______ c. Being friends is part of staying in love
_______ d. Making love is important for staying in love

4. Which of the following things (if any) would you like more of in your relationship?

_______a. More intimate conversation
_______b. Ability to deal with our differences
_______c. A stronger friendship between us
_______d. More lovemaking

5. Which one of the above would you like to have the *most* in your marriage?

(Example: a stronger friendship)

____

6. What would it mean to you to have more of this quality in your relationship? (Example: I wish we were better friends so we would be able to relax more with each other.)

____

____

____

— 13 —
To Know You Is to Love You

Did you know that one of the meanings for the word "know" in the Bible is to "make love"? So, when we read in Genesis that Adam "knew his wife," it means that he got to know her *really* well.

And though we no longer use the word *know* in that sense, there is something beautiful about considering lovemaking as a type of knowing. When we are close both emotionally *and* physically, we have achieved true intimacy. We all long to be known, especially by the person we have sworn our lives to.

Here are four strategies for getting to know each another better:

a. Take time to talk
b. Look at each other
c. Grab a few minutes
d. Make some sweet, sweet love

This chapter has one exercise for each of these strategies. The following exercise is for talking to each other in a meaningful way.

"Ten Questions to Love" Exercise

With your spouse, take turns asking the following questions of one another. One person asks the first question and the other person answers.

Then the other person asks the next question and the other person answers. Do not interrupt your spouse. Listen while they are talking, without any distractions. After they are done, you may ask clarifying questions, such as "do you mean ..." or "why do you feel that way?"
You may not doubt them or act cynical, though. You must accept whatever they say.

Please note that these are fun questions to ask again in a month or two and see if your answers have changed!

If you would like a downloadable version of the questions, go to this page:

https://secondmarriage.xyz/get-the-ten-questions-to-love/

Ten Questions to Love

1. What was the most challenging part of your day?

2. What was your favourite part of last weekend?

3. What is your favourite quality about yourself?

4. What one thing would you most like to change about yourself?

5. Who is your favourite person in my family, and why?

6. What is the best gift you have ever received?

7. What would you like to be doing in five years?

8. What would you like to learn?

9. How are you feeling right now?

10. How could I make you happier in the coming week?

"Look at Me!" Exercise

If you have access to the Internet, you may want to watch the following video together before you complete the task. Title: *Couples Stare at Each Other for 4 Minutes Straight* | Glamour

https://www.youtube.com/watch?v=ONYlKmdylXg

This next exercise is designed to get you looking at your spouse. It is very simple, but I think you may also find it quite powerful!

1. Decide on a time that you are both available and simply look at each other for two minutes straight. Do not talk, and try not to laugh!

2. Write about your experience here. Did you feel awkward at first? Did you feel closer to your spouse after doing this?

____

____

____

"Grab a Few Minutes" Exercise

In a second marriage, especially if it is a stepfamily situation, it is often hard to find time to be together. We may feel bad that we don't go on regular dates. This next exercise is designed to squeeze in some more time together, even when you are both on busy schedules.

1. Do you find it hard to find "couple time"? YES / NO / SOMETIMES

2. Do you go on dates as often as you would like? YES / NO / SOMETIMES

3. If you need more time together and dates are hard to come by, try grabbing a few minutes during your day, and making the most of them. Write down two times where you could "grab" ten to fifteen minutes to spend together and make it special.

Example: When we eat breakfast in the morning.

Time #1: ____

Time #2: ____

If you would like more ideas on this topic, check out the following resource:

11 Ideas For Connecting with Your Spouse: When You Don't Have Any Time.

You can find this attractive, fun download for free at:

http://secondmarriage.xyz/connection-ideas/

"Make Some Sweet, Sweet Love" Exercise

1. How often do you make love with your spouse?

_______ a. Daily or almost daily
_______ c. 2-3 times a week
_______ d. Once a week
_______ e. 2-3 times a month
_______ f. Once a month
_______ g. Less than once a month

2. Are you content with the amount of lovemaking in your relationship?

YES / NO / NOT SURE

3. Ask your partner if they are content with the amount of lovemaking in your relationship. What do they say?

YES / NO / NOT SURE

4. If either one of you is not satisfied with your frequency of lovemaking, are you willing to try to make adjustments?

YES / NO / UNSURE

5. If you answered YES, plan a time in your schedule that would work for both of you. Planning for intimate times may not sound romantic but when your schedule is hectic, it might be the only way that it happens.

Example: We will try to make love instead of watching television on Wednesday evenings.

____

____

–14 –
You're My Best Friend

Do you remember the older couples who were still "feeling the love" back in Chapter 12? One of the characteristics that most of these couples shared was that they were good friends with each other.

How do we become better friends with our mate? Well, the first step is to determine how good our friendship is *now* by examining what it means to be a true friend. Let's look at some of the qualities of good friends.

First of all, most friendships start out over something the two people have in common. Whether it's a shared love of the hometown football team or a passion for shopping, friends usually do activities together. While they are going out, friends usually like to have some laughs.

A good friend is always loyal and doesn't speak behind someone's back. And a real friend accepts the other person just as they are. The following questions are to measure how good the friendship is with your spouse.

Friendship Self-assessment

1. Do you consider you and your spouse to be good friends? Why or why not?

____

____

2. What do you think is the most important characteristic of a good friend?

____

3. Do you usually demonstrate this quality to your partner? YES / NO

4. Do they usually demonstrate this quality to you? YES / NO

5. Using a scale of 1-5 (with 1 being very poor to 5 being excellent) rate your relationship on the following characteristics:

a. Sharing things in common: 1 2 3 4 5

b. Sharing laughter: 1 2 3 4 5

c. Loyalty: 1 2 3 4 5

d. Acceptance: 1 2 3 4 5

6. Which **one** of the following characteristics of friendship, if any, do you think needs the most work?

a. Sharing things in common: _________

b. Sharing laughter: _________

c. Loyalty: _________

d. Acceptance: _________

7. Write out a commitment to work on that one aspect in your relationship.

Example: I will try to take time to laugh more with my spouse.

____

— 15 —
Handling Conflict

Conflict is a part of every marriage and the complications of a second marriage make disagreements even more likely. Sometimes we need better skills in navigating the conflicts that arise.

"Reasons That We Argue" Questions

When we have disagreements, it is sometimes hard to discern the real reason behind the conflict. Understanding the reasons for our conflict can go a long way toward solving it. The following are common reasons that people find themselves in disagreement.

1. For each question, answer if you think this reason applies to you. (First, we will look at our own actions, and in the next set of questions, we will examine our spouse's actions.) Answer using one of the following:

YES (Y) / NO (N) / MAYBE (M) NOT APPLICABLE (NA)

a. Do you sometimes feel left out of your spouse's decisions? ________

b. Do you ever feel left out by other members of the stepfamily? _______

c. Do you sometimes feel frustrated with your spouse's actions? __________

d. Do you ever feel frustrated with things you have no control over? __________

e. Do you ever bring up issues when one or both of you are already feeling stressed? __________

f. Do you ever bring up issues when one or both of you are feeling hungry or exhausted? _________

g. Do you complain negatively to your spouse about what they are doing?

____

h. If a problem is not solved immediately, do you continue to press the issue over and over again until your spouse gives in? _________

i. Do you immediately defend yourself when your spouse brings up an issue?

____

2. Out of the answers for which you answered YES OR MAYBE, which one do you do the most?

Example: I get frustrated with my spouse's actions a lot.

____

3. Name one situation where you have seen the factor named above in action.

Example: I tend to get frustrated when the custody schedule changes at the last minute and then I eventually blow up. This happened last weekend.

____

____

____

4. For each factor, answer if you think this reason applies to your spouse (or if you feel comfortable, ask him/her to answer the questions.)

Answer YES (Y) / NO (N) / NOT SURE (NS) NOT APPLICABLE (NA)

a. Does your spouse sometimes feel left out of your decisions? __________

b. Does your partner ever feel left out by other members of the stepfamily?

____

c. Does your spouse sometimes feel frustrated with your actions?

____

d. Does your mate ever feel frustrated with things they have no control over? __________

e. Does your mate bring up issues when one or both of you are already feeling stressed? __________

f. Does your partner ever bring up issues when one or both of you are feeling hungry or exhausted?

____

g. Do they complain negatively to you about what you are doing? __________

h. If a problem is not solved immediately, do they continue to press the issue over and over again until you react? _________

5. Out of the answers for which you answered YES OR MAYBE, which one does your spouse do the most?

Example: He gets frustrated with my actions very often.

____

6. Name one situation where you have seen the factor named above in action.

Example: My partner tends to get frustrated when the custody schedule changes at the last minute, and then she eventually blows up. This happened last weekend.

____

____

____

7. Write down (or draw) one thing you learned about conflict in your marriage from this exercise.

"Talk to Me" Exercise

1. a. Write up to two things that are issues in your marriage right now.

Examples might be: housework issues, money problems, discipline disagreements, ex-issues, personality differences.

Issue
#1____

Issue
#2____

b. For each issue, write down something you might say (or have said) to your spouse in anger or frustration.

Example: You always wake me up when you get up early to go to work! Don't you care that I need to get my sleep?

2. Now, for each thing that you have written, write something that is more positive.

Example: I just love getting that extra bit of sleep in the morning after you leave for work. Would you mind being a bit quieter, so I can indulge myself a little?

Issue #1: ______________________________

a. Something you might say/have said:

____

____

b. A better way of saying it:

____

____

Issue #2:

____

a. Something you might say/have said:

____

____

b. A better way of saying it:

____

____

– 16 –
The Dance of Opposites

Have you ever wanted to scream because your partner just doesn't understand you? Do you ever wonder if you and your spouse are just too different? If you and your mate sometimes seem like complete opposites, don't despair. Help is on the way! This chapter is for you.

Personality differences are a reality in most marriages. Even the most seemingly compatible couples will find remarkable differences between them as they get to know each other. Ironically, we seem to be attracted to our opposite, perhaps seeking something we are missing in ourselves.

To assess your areas of difference, I have created a four-part personality test, based on work from Carl Jung[1] and the Myers-Briggs personality tests.

Personality Differences Part One
Extrovert/Introvert

Answer the following questions about yourself.

1. Which is truer of you?

______a. I like my quiet time.
______b. I crave being around people.

1. Carl Jung, 1971. *Psychological Types, Collected Works of C.G. Jung*

2. Which is truer of you?

______a. I get stressed if I am around people too much.
______b. I get stressed if I am alone too much.

3. Which is truer of you?

______a. Large groups of people make me feel exhausted!
______b. Large groups of people make me come alive!

If you answered more *a*'s than *b*'s, **you are an introvert**. This means you primarily get your energy from being alone.

If you answered more *b*'s than *a*'s, **you are an extrovert**. This means that you primarily get your energy from being around people.

4. Are you an introvert or an extrovert?

____

Answer the following questions about your spouse (or get him/her to take the quiz)

5. Which is truer of your spouse?

______ a. They like their quiet time.
______ b. They crave being around people.

6. Which is truer of your mate?

______ a. They get depressed if they are alone too much.
______ b. They get stressed if they are around people too much.

7. Which is truer of your partner?

______ a. Large groups of people make them feel exhausted!
______ b. Large groups of people make them come alive!

If they scored more *a*'s than *b*'s, **you are married to an introvert**. This means they get their energy primarily from being alone.

If they scored more *b*'s than *a*'s, **you are married to an extrovert**. This means that they get their energy primarily from being around people.

Is your spouse an introvert or an extrovert?

____

8. Are you and your spouse the same or different in this area?

THE SAME / DIFFERENT

Introverts need the following:

- Environments that allow for some quiet time
- Time alone away from everyone
- Time to wind down after a busy period

Extroverts need the following:

- To be around people
- Time to socialize with groups
- Excitement and outward stimulation

9. Do you feel that your introvert/extrovert needs are being met in your life?

YES / NO

10. If you answered NO, which needs are not being met?

____

____

11. What is something you would like to do to try to better meet your introvert/extrovert needs?

____

____

____

____

12. Do you think your spouse's introvert/extrovert needs are being met?

YES / NO

12. If you answered NO, which needs are not being met? How so?

____

____

13. What is something you could do to help or encourage your spouse to meet their introvert/extrovert needs?

____

____

Ways to Complement Each Other

- Extroverts can take on more of the socializing role and shield the introvert.
- Introverts can help the extrovert to take time to slow down and relax.

14. If the two of you are different in this area, how are your differences actually a strength in your marriage?

____

____

15. If the two of you are the same in this area, how has this similarity strengthened your marriage?

____

____

Personality Differences Part Two: Practical / Idea-Based

Answer the following questions about yourself.

1. Which is truer of you?

______a. You like talking about abstract ideas.
______b. You like talking about projects you are working on.

2. Which is truer of you?

______ a. You tend to question *why* something must be done.
______ b. You like to "just do it" without questioning the reason.

3. Which is truer of you?

______ a. You tend to be less observant than others.
______ b. You tend to be more observant than others.

If you answered more *a*'s than *b*'s, you are more **idea-based than practical.**

If you answered more *b*'s than *a*'s, you are more **practical than idea-based.**

4. Are you more idea-based or practical?

____

Answer the following questions about your spouse (or get them to take the quiz)

5. Which is truer of your partner?

______a. They like talking about abstract ideas.
______b. They like talking about projects they are working on.

6. Which is truer of your partner?

______ a. They tend to question why something must be done.
______ b. They like to "just do it" without questioning the reason.

7. Which is truer of your partner?

______ a. They tend to be less observant than others.
______ b. They tend to be more observant than others.

If your spouse has more *a*'s, they are more **idea-based than practical.**

If they have more *b*'s, they are more **practical than idea-based.**

8. Is your mate more idea-based or practical?

____

9. Are the two of you the same or different in this area?

SAME / DIFFERENT

Practical people have the following strengths:

- Observation skills
- Hands-on activities

Idea-based people have the following strengths:

- Understands abstract things
- Ability to see things that are not immediately apparent

Ways to Complement Each Other

- A practical person can help the idea-based person to see a more realistic viewpoint.

- The idea-based person can help the practical person have more of a long-term vision and purpose.

10. If you are different, how do you think this could be a strength for the two of you?

Example: Because my wife is more practical than me, she helps me stay on budget.

____

____

11. If you are the same type, what is something that you share together related to this strength?

Example: We both love working on home improvement projects together.

____

Personality Differences Part Three: Thinking / Feeling

Answer the following questions about yourself.

1. Which is truer of you?

______ a. I love to figure out the plot of a movie.
______ b. I love to analyze the motives of a movie character.

2. Which is truer of you?

______ a. I don't usually take things personally.
______ b. I often take things personally.

3. Which is truer of you?

______ a. My decisions are rarely affected by my emotions.
______ b. My decisions are often affected by my emotions.

If you answered more *a*'s than *b*'s, you are more of a **thinker** when it comes to decisions.

If you answered more *b*'s than a's, you are more of a **feeler** when it comes to decisions.

4. Are you more of a thinker or a feeler when it comes to decisions?

____

Answer the following questions about your spouse (or get them to take the quiz)

5. Which is truer of your spouse?

_______ a. They love to figure out the plot of a movie.
_______ b. They love to analyze the motives of a movie character.

6. Which is truer of your spouse?

_______ a. They don't usually take things personally.
_______ b. They sometimes take things personally.

7. Which is truer of your spouse?

_______ a. Their decisions are rarely affected by their emotions.
_______ b. Their decisions are often affected by their emotions.

If they have more a's than *b*'s, they are more of a **thinker,** when it comes to decisions.

If they answered more *b*'s than *a*'s, they are more of a **feeler**, when it comes to decisions.

8. Is your spouse more of a thinker or a feeler when it comes to decisions?

____

9. Are the two of you different or the same in this area?

Same / Different

First of all, please note that, of course, all people are thinkers and feelers! This aspect of personality refers only to how we primarily make decisions: first through thinking, or first through feeling.

Thinker people have the following strengths:

- Ability to make tough decisions when necessary
- Ability to not be manipulated by others

Feeler people have the following strengths:

- Ability to see people's emotional needs
- Ability to have mercy even if a person doesn't "deserve it."

Ways to Complement Each Other

- Thinkers can help their partner stay calm when there is an emotional situation in their life.
- Feelers can help point out the emotional component of a situation that the other partner may not pick up on.

10. If you are different, how is this difference a strength in your relationship?

Example: My feeler partner helps me understand why my children are acting out.

____

____

11. If you and your spouse are the same type, how is this similarity a strength in your relationship?

Example: My spouse and I usually agree on our major decisions.

____

Personality Differences Part Four
Structured / Open-Ended

Answer the following questions about yourself.

1. Which is truer of you?

________ a. I tend to plan everything carefully.
________ b. I prefer to go moment by moment.

2. Which is truer of you?

______ a. I tend to keep things neat and tidy.
______ b. I struggle with being messy.

3. Which is truer of you?
______ a. I am usually a bit early.
______ b. I am more often running late.

If you answered more *a*'s than *b*'s, you are more **structured.**

If you answered more *b*'s than *a*'s, you are more **open-ended**.

4. Are you more structured or open-ended?

____

Answer the following questions about your spouse. (Or ask them to take the quiz)

5. Which is truer of your spouse?

______ a. They tend to plan everything carefully.
______ b. They tend to go moment by moment.

6. Which is truer of your spouse?

______ a. They tend to keep their things neat and tidy.
______ b. They struggle with being messy.

7. Which is truer of your spouse?

______ a. They are usually a bit early.
______ b. They are running a bit late.

If they answered more *a*'s than *b*'s, they are more **structured.**

If they answered more *b*'s than *a*'s, they are more **open-ended.**

8. Is your spouse more structured or open-ended?

____

Are the two of you the same or different in this area?

Same / Different

Those that are open-ended need the following:

- Freedom to be flexible with their time
- To be able to enjoy the process of what they are doing

Those that are more structured need the following:

- A regular routine
- The means to get things done

Ways to Complement Each Other

- Structured people can encourage the more open-ended person to be more disciplined in finishing tasks.

- Open-ended people can encourage the structured person to be more open to adventure.

10. If you are different as a couple in this area, how is this difference a strength?

Example: My husband pushes me to try our holidays in places where I would never go on my own.

____

____

11. If you and your partner are the same in this area, how has this strengthened your relationship?

Example: We both love sticking to a routine and accomplishing things together.

____

____

— 17 —
Becoming a Family

Please note that the next two chapters are for stepfamilies, especially those with children still at home. If you and your partner did not have kids when you married, move ahead to Chapter 19.

When a couple remarries, it is an exciting new phase of their lives. It is often, however, much less exciting for the little people in their lives.

Be patient with your children. They may still be grieving the ending of their old family and the way things used to be. In addition, children are now forced to continually adjust as they come and go from your home.

The forming of a stepfamily is similar to two companies merging. When two companies merge, the newly found entity must decide which traditions, rules and practices will be brought in from each company. These next questions will encourage you to examine the routines and rituals in your family.

Reflection Questions

1. Do you have any routines with the children now? If so, what are they? Write them down here. Remember that these don't have to be big things. Routines are simply things that you do on a regular basis.

____

____

____

2. Now, ask the kids what they think your family's routines are and record them here.

____

____

____

____

3. Were you surprised by any of the routines that the kids mentioned? Why or why not?

____

____

4. Ask the kids what new routine they would like to develop together as a family. It could be something serious or goofy. The important thing is that you do it together! Write about it here.

____

____

____

— 18 —
Becoming a Parent by Marriage

If you became a stepparent when you married your spouse, this chapter is for you. If you are not a stepparent, you can skip ahead to Chapter 19.

Becoming a parent to someone else's children is one of the hardest jobs in the world. One of the reasons for this difficulty is that you are trying to do the work of a parent without the automatic authority of a biological parent.

Understanding your role is very tricky when you step into a family. You haven't been around long enough to be respected as the biological parent, but sometimes you are put in a position where some form of discipline is necessary.

Making things even more difficult is something called a "loyalty bind." This is the feeling of guilt that children experience when they like you but they think loving you will mean they are being disloyal to their other biological parent. This helps to explain why a child may seem to be warming up to you one minute and then distant the next time you see them.
Loyalty binds are often reinforced by the other parent, who may be struggling with having another adult in the child's life.

Reflection Questions

1. Were you familiar with the term "loyalty bind"? YES / NO

2 If you were not familiar with this term, does knowing about it help you understand the behaviour of the children in your family better? If so, in what way?

____

____

____

3. Do you think the children may sometimes feel a loyalty bind? If so, describe what that looks like.

____

____

____

One of the greatest challenges for a new stepparent is to develop a sense of trust with their stepchild. Here are four strategies that will help to develop that sense of trust. If you are interested in having these concepts spelled in a fun, attractive format, I would love to offer you my complementary mini ebook on this topic which can be found on my website at:

https://secondmarriage.xyz/four-gifts-book/

I have also written a full book on ways that stepmoms can connect with their stepchildren called:

16 *Gifts From a Stepmom: Encouragement for the Blended Family Journey*

You can find it on Amazon in both Kindle and print form at the following place:

https://www.amazon.com/16-Gifts-Stepmom-Encouragement-Blended/dp/1999028619

Four Ways to Bond with Your Stepchild

1. One of the most powerful ways to get to know anyone is simply to listen. Be curious and interested in learning about your stepchild and his world.

2. Another effective way of bonding is to do day-to-day activities with them. Invite them to go grocery shopping with you or to help with a meal.

3. Finally, in order to really gain the trust of the new people in your life, be sure to honour both of their parents. You can do this in two ways. First of all, never speak poorly of the other biological parent (the one that you are not with.)

4. Secondly, make sure that they have "alone time" with your partner. Sure, they need to bond with you, but they also need to know that they can maintain the relationship they have with your spouse, even when you are around.

Reflection Questions

1. Which of the following strategies did you find the most helpful?

______ a. Listening
______ b. Doing activities together
______ c. Honouring their other biological parent
______ d. Allowing them time alone with your partner

2. What strategy do you need to work on the most (if any)?

____

3. What is one action you could start doing right away?

Example: I could start listening more when my stepchild talks about his day.

____

____

— 19 —

Taking Care of Yourself

As we have discussed throughout this book, second marriages carry extra pressures that can cause additional stress. Therefore, it is essential to remind yourself who *you* are in the midst of your situation. You need to have things in your life that are separate from being a wife, or a husband, and are just "you."

Know that you may have to fight for this time alone. It won't necessarily come easy. You may have to battle guilt and overwhelm. Remember, though, that when we strengthen the essence of who we are, we have more to bring to the relationship. Part of meeting your own needs is taking time to do something that you thoroughly enjoy.

Reflection Questions

1. Do you ever feel like you are losing sight of who you are within your marriage?

YES / NO / NOT SURE

2. What activities or pursuits do you have in your life that remind you that you are still "you"?

____

____

____

Do this exercise if you would like to be creative. In this space, draw or paste images of things that bring you joy and represent who you are as an individual. Create a collage, which is one picture created from many different smaller images.

– 20 –
When You Feel Lonely

Do you feel like you are the only one in the world who is struggling like you are? Does it seem like no one could ever relate? Being in a second marriage, with all its complications, can be lonely because we feel like no one understands. It is reassuring to know that although you may feel alone, there are many others in similar situations.

If you are in a stepfamily situation, you may find it to be a lonely place because stepfamilies can be so divisive at the beginning. The blended family is the process of taking strangers and making them into family and this takes time. In the meantime, it is easy for all parties to feel misunderstood and isolated.

When we are alone, one of the most powerful ways to break through the loneliness is to reach out. We are all social beings and we need each other. If you tend to cut yourself off when things are tough, I want to encourage you to reach out even if it is uncomfortable.

Reflection Questions

1. Do you ever feel like no one could possibly understand what you are going through? YES / NO

2. Do you ever feel lonely being in a stepfamily? YES / NO

3. Have you cut yourself off from friends and family because of the struggles you are experiencing? YES / NO

4. If you answered YES above, who are some of the people you have cut yourself off from?

____

____

____

This next exercise is for anyone who has cut themself off from others because of the struggles they are experiencing.

"I'm So Lonely" Exercise

Sometime in the next week, contact someone that you haven't spoken to in a while. This could be a friend, family member or former colleague. Lightly share a bit about your life and listen to what is happening with them. If they are in your city, and you feel comfortable doing so, invite them for coffee or some other event.

Note: If you are reading this during the quarantine time, you will, of course, need to follow the guidelines for socializing during this time.

Write about your experience here:

1. Who did you contact?

____

2. What is your relationship to this person?

Example: friend

3. How long has it been since you last contacted this person?

____

4. How did you contact them?

Example: through Facebook

____

5. What did you talk about?

____

____

— 21 —

Getting Help

As we have discussed throughout this book, second marriage is often more complicated than marriage the first time around. Sometimes we need to talk to someone in person who can help us sort out the issues. The next exercise is designed to help you determine if you might be in need of some outside help.

"Help us!" Exercise

1. Have you ever considered counselling or other help for your marriage?

YES / NO

2. Have you ever been in marriage counselling with your current spouse?

YES / NO

3. What was the main reason that you considered counselling or other marriage help?

____

____

4. The following factors are reasons that people may go to a counsellor or a marriage coach to help them out. The more of these factors you have in your relationship, the more likely it is that you may need some outside help.

_______ a. You argue and fight constantly.

_______ b. You or your partner still need healing from your past.

_______ c. Your children are being affected by the conflict.

_______ d. You are having serious problems with communication.

_______ e. You want to invest in your marriage to prevent future problems

_______ f. You are dealing with adultery, addictions or abuse

5. How many of these factors applied to you? _____________

When you are considering getting marriage assistance, it is very important to find the right person. Not everyone will be a fit for you and your spouse. For this reason, many marriage therapists and coaches will offer a complementary session to find out if they are a fit. On the next page, you will find a list of questions that you can ask of a counsellor or coach on your first session. If you are not comfortable with the person, you are free to walk away and find someone else.

The following set of questions can be photocopied, so that you can take it with you to the session. It is also available for printing at:

https://secondmarriage.xyz/counsellorquestions/

Counsellor Questions

1. What kind of approach do you take to counselling/coaching. (If they say something but you don't understand the term, ask them to explain.)

____

____

2. (This is for people of faith.) Faith is an important part of my life. Are you comfortable dealing with matters of faith in our sessions?

____

3. How would we decide what to talk about and our goals for counselling/coaching?

____

____

5. What is your professional background?

____

6. What do you like about the job of counselling/coaching?

____

7. What is your experience/background in dealing with couples in second marriages and stepfamilies?

____

Where to Find Help

Sometimes finding help for your marriage can be a difficult process. Here are some ideas for looking for more help for your relationship.

1. Check with local churches: Some churches have a counsellor on staff or a list of recommended resources.
2. Ask friends that you know who have had struggles if they have any seen anyone that is helpful. (This can be potentially awkward, so be sure you are close enough to ask this type of question.)
3. Find a marriage coach, who can also help you find solutions for the issues in your relationship.
4. I have a list of recommended resources on my website, and there is a section of programs you can access.Have a look at this page:

https://secondmarriage.xyz/recommended-resources8587/

I also offer coaching services for couples with a history or stepmoms. To read more about my coaching services, see this page:

https://secondmarriage.xyz/relationship-coaching/

— 22 —
How Are You Doing?

Congratulations! You made it all the way through the book. I am absolutely thrilled you were able to make this journey for yourself, your marriage and your family. It has been a lot of work. Way to go!

First of all, I hope you celebrate! Working your marriage is an investment for the future and definitely worthy of celebration. Before you go, take a few minutes with the exercise below and see how far you have come.

1. At the beginning of this book, you identified the top three priorities for growth in your marriage. Go back to that page now (found at the end of Chapter One) and write down the three areas:

1.____

2. ____

3. ____

2. Now, for each area, write down what you have learned or how you have grown through the process of going through the workbook.

Example: 1. Learning to forgive: I realized I hadn't forgiven my ex-wife, and I am working on trying to forgive her.

Example 2. Handling conflict better: I am handling arguments more constructively now.

Priority 1: ____________________

What you learned / how you grew in this area:

____

____

Priority 2: ____________________

What you learned/how you grew in this area:

____

____

Priority 3: ____________________

What you learned/how you grew in this area:

____

____

Thank You

Thank you for having the courage to work on your marriage with this workbook. I truly hope it was healing and helpful to you. If you would like to explore the topics in this book in greater depth, with more stories, examples and research, check out my book, *Happily Ever After Again: Hope, Healing & Love for Second Marriages,* found on Amazon.

To stay in touch, join my mailing list at:

https://secondmarriage.xyz/sign-up-here

And now, I have just one favour to ask you. Would you mind helping to spread the word about this book by leaving a review on Amazon or Goodreads? It would mean so much to me, as I read every single review and appreciate them so much.

Your review also will help spread this message of encouragement to the world. You can review at Amazon at the link below:

http://www.Amazon.com/gp/customer-reviews/write-a-review.html?asin=B0892RM5FN

Acknowledgements

Thank you to the LORD Jesus Christ, who is my everything.

Thank you to Paula Pietrobono and Debra Butterfield, the two editors whose patience and attention to detail has shaped this document into something clear and readable. You ladies are amazing!

Thank you to Shelley Hitz and the Christian Book Academy for your support and encouragement in my writing.

Thank you to all the writers and researchers who paved the way on the subjects of remarriage, divorce and blended families.

Also By Sharilee Swaity

Marriage the second time around is more complicated. You are no longer as young or as naive. Hurts from the past still taunt you. Things are more complicated.

But it is never too late to gain a new vision of your relationship, the way it was meant to be! This book is an encouraging read that will make you feel hopeful for your relationship. Pick up this engaging book today and gain new hope for your marriage.

Being a stepmom is kind of like being a secret millionaire. You have a lot to give but no one realizes it yet. It is difficult to connect with the kids who are now a permanent part of your life.

This book will give you tools and strategies for making genuine connections. Get your copy of this volume today, a special book written especially for stepmothers.

Appendix: Facilitator's Guide

This workbook may be used in a group or marriage counselling setting. Depending on your circumstances and time constraints, you may also wish to have the participants purchase the accompanying book, *Happily Ever After Again: Hope, Healing & Love for Second Marriages*, which gives more detail and background concerning the concepts taught in the workbook. Then, have the participants read the corresponding chapters weekly.

Note about sensitive topics: This workbook has some very sensitive issues (such as dealing with insecurities and the difficulties of stepfamily dynamics.) Let the participants know they only need to share what they feel comfortable sharing. It is important that everyone feels emotionally safe in working through these issues. Have couples (if applicable) sit together and share mostly with each other.

12-WEEK STUDY PLAN

The following is a suggested plan for using this book for a 12-week study plan. Please feel free to modify this plan for your own teaching situation.

Week One: Introduction & Chapter 1
Week Two: Chapter 2
Week Three: Chapters 3 & 4
Week Four: Chapters 5 & 6
Week Five: Chapters 7& 8
Week Six: Chapters 9 & 10
Week Seven: Chapter 11 & 12
Week Eight: Chapter 13
Week Nine: Chapters 14 & 15
Week Ten: Chapter 16
Week Eleven: Chapter 17 & 18
Week Twelve: Chapters 19 — 22

HAPPILY EVER AFTER AGAIN STUDY
12 WEEK SCHEDULE

DAY OF WEEK:______________________________

TIME: ______________PLACE: ___________________________

Week	Date	Subject	Chapters from Workbook (and book if you choose to use it.)	Questions/Comments for When You Are Reading Ahead
One		Introduction / The Decision to Marry	Introduction/Chapter 1	
Two		Rediscovering the Why for Your Marriage	Chapter 2	
Three		The Complexities of Second Marriages	Chapters 3 & 4	
Four		New Perspective and Why Healing is Difficult	Chapters 5 & 6	
Five		Steps to Healing – Part One	Chapters 7 & 8	
Six		Steps to Healing – Part Two	Chapters 9 & 10	
Seven		Accepting Your Story and Loving Your Spouse	Chapters 11 & 12	
Eight		Getting to Know Your Spouse	Chapter 13	
Nine		Friendship and Conflict	Chapters 14 & 15	
Ten		Personality Differences	Chapter 16	
Eleven		Stepfamily Issues	Chapters 17 & 18	
Twelve		Final Steps	Chapters 19-22	

Customizable Study Plan

This is a plan is a way to customize the experience to the specific needs of your group if you have less than twelve weeks to complete the study.

Note: This section is a bit complicated. If you would like more direction on how to do this, please feel free to check a video where I explain how to do this, at the following address:

https://secondmarriage.xyz/facilitators-guide/

If you have any questions on how it works, you can also email me at admin@secondmarriage.xyz.

Step One: Have all participants fill out the Priority Assessment two times: first in the workbook and then by copying the answers onto the Priority Assessment Handout. Have them hand in their priority assessment to you.

Step Two: After the group is over, add up all the priority assessments using the **group priority sheet.** Certain chapters (Intro, Ch. 1, 2, 13, 16, 21 and 22) are listed as KEEP. These are chapters that I recommend doing for all groups. There are eight other sections of two chapters each. When you are adding up the priorities, add priorities for both chapters of that section.

(i.e. For chapters 3 & 4, you will add up what each participant put as a priority for both chapters 3 and 4.)

Step Three: After you have totaled the priorities, rank them according to the totals from 1-8.

Step Four: Determine how many sessions you will be skipping. Note: If you are having 12 sessions, I would recommend using the 12-week study plan. If it is less than 12 sessions, subtract the number of sessions you are having from 12.

(i.e. If you are having an eight-week class, subtract eight from twelve and you get four skipped sections.)

Step Five: Cross off the least ranked sections with a pen or a pencil. REMEMBER TO KEEP THE SECTIONS MARKED "KEEP."

(i.e. If you are having an eight-week class, you will be skipping the four least ranked sessions, with the exception of the KEEP sessions.

Step Six: Go through the workbook in order, leaving out the skipped sections. Note that Week One will be the introduction. Week Two will be Chapters 1 & 2. The last week will be Chapters 21 & 22.

Step Seven: Invite participants to finish up the other chapters on their own time after they are done.

Group Priority Assessment

Please see instructions above for how to use this chart.

Date	Subject	Chapters from Workbook (and book if you choose to use it.)	Questions/Comments for When You Are Reading Ahead
	Introduction / The Decision to Marry	Introduction/Chapter 1	
	Rediscovering the Why for Your Marriage	Chapter 2	
	The Complexities of Second Marriages	Chapters 3 & 4	
	New Perspective and Why Healing is Difficult	Chapters 5 & 6	
	Steps to Healing – Part One	Chapters 7 & 8	
	Steps to Healing – Part Two	Chapters 9 & 10	
	Accepting Your Story and Loving Your Spouse	Chapters 11 & 12	
	Getting to Know Your Spouse	Chapter 13	
	Friendship and Conflict	Chapters 14 & 15	
	Personality Differences	Chapter 16	
	Stepfamily Issues	Chapters 17 & 18	
	Final Steps	Chapters 19-22	

HAPPILY EVER AFTER AGAIN STUDY

________ WEEK SCHEDULE

DAY OF WEEK:________________________________

TIME: ______________PLACE: ___________________________

Week	Date	Subject	Chapters To Read Ahead (if applicable)	Questions/Comments for when you read ahead
One		Introduction	N/A	
Two		The Decision to Marry	Chapters 1 and 2	

Suggested Weekly Lesson Plans

The following are two suggested weekly lessons plan to follow so you have a similar class every week. Feel free to make these your own and use the book in whatever way works for you. Most weeks, you will be covering two chapters, so class can be divided to accommodate that. For one-chapter weeks, simply divide the chapter in half.

If you are using the book *Happily Ever After Again: Hope, Healing & Love for Second Marriages* as a supplement, I would have students read the corresponding chapters ahead of time and schedule time at the beginning of class to discuss the book.

Suggested Time: 90 minutes (with break)

I will use an example to illustrate a possible class schedule.

7:00-7:20: Open: chat and getting settled. Go over questions/comments from homework and readings.

7:20-7:45: Go through material from first chapter. Whatever isn't done, ask students to do for homework. If they are not able to do homework, just get done what you can get done.

7:45-8:00: Break

8:00-8:25: Go through material from second chapter. Whatever isn't done, assign for homework.

8:25-8:30: Review homework and readings for next week.

The following lesson plan is if you are not using the accompanying book as a supplement and would like to finish the course in an hour.

Suggested Time: 60 minutes

7:00-7:05: Open: chat and getting settled.

7:05-7:30: Go through material from first chapter. Whatever isn't done, ask students to do for homework. If they are not able to do homework, just get done what you can get done.

7:30-7:55: Go through material from second chapter.

7:55-8:00: Introduce topic for next week. Say good-byes.

Facilitator's chapter notes

Please note that these facilitator's chapter notes are available as a free download at the following web address:

https://secondmarriage.xyz/facilitators-guide/

Introduction

Start by welcoming everyone. You can read the "our story" together and then discuss if any of them relate to the story. Did they have a small wedding? Did they feel ill-prepared for the complications that lie ahead?

Then, go to the assessments and three main goal section and have each participant complete on their own. If you are doing the customized study plan, see instructions for the priority assessment. Be sure to go over the instructions carefully for both assessments and the three main goals.

Chapter One

I would recommend reading through this chapter together and having participants fill in the questions as you go. Some of the answers are meant to have humour so feel free to have fun with it!

Chapter Two

This is an important chapter. I recommend going through the first part as a group, giving plenty of time to write down answers and reflect on the answers. If you are having a break, I would suggest breaking it up before you write the letter. You could hand out paper to do the letters or have them use the book. Try to get everyone to write a letter, using the format suggested. They can add more content to the letter. The example given is pretty "bare-bones." If someone needs help with grammar and spelling, they can ask you or ask the group.

Chapter Three

I would suggest going through the first question together as a class. You can read aloud and ask others to read aloud, too, to break it up. Make sure it is clear that they need to pick either a, b, c, d, or *e*, for each ex-partner the two of you deal with as a couple.

You don't need to read the "Complicating Factors" out loud. Just let the students fill that out on their own. At the end, it would be fun to ask each person what their number is.

The questions after the checklist are something you could try together. This could be a chance to share and get to know each other. Gauge it by how comfortable they feel in sharing. It can be therapeutic to hear that you are not the only one going through something. Always make it clear, though, that they are never obligated to share.

Chapter Four

I would recommend reading this chapter aloud (either you or the other class members), giving people time to fill in the answers as you go. Give time at the end to write down how they are feeling about their marriage in general. If they prefer, you could also tell them to do that part at home.

Chapter Five

This chapter has a long introduction, so I would recommend having other people help you read. Then, class members can fill in the exercises by themselves. If they feel comfortable, this can be nice to have people read one of their answers. It can help them realize they are not alone.

Chapter Six

This chapter is quite sensitive, so you will want to be gentle with people with this session. Explain that you are not diagnosing anyone — these are just signs that someone "may" be experiencing grief in a particular area. To be sure, they would need to see a counsellor or a doctor.

Chapter Seven

This chapter is quite sensitive. I would suggest reading the first part out loud, to get your definitions clear and then letting participants complete the last questions on their own.

Chapter Eight

This chapter is about repeating patterns from the past. It may be uncomfortable for some participants but encourage them to try to see if any of their habits are repeating. This can even happen unconsciously. Second married couples often do this without even realizing they are doing so!

Chapter Nine

This chapter has two distinct parts. The first part is on forgiveness. This can be very intense. Emphasize that the goal of today is to be willing to forgive — not necessarily forgive, which take a long time to work through. Do not put any pressure — but just by doing this exercise, you are inviting the participants to consider forgiveness.

The second part of the exercise is meant to be fun, and a light touch after some intense work. If you want, go to the following page, where you can get a copy of *11 Ideas for Connecting With Your Spouse When You Don't Have Any Time.*

https://secondmarriage.xyz/connection-ideas/

As a facilitator, you have my permission to photocopy this resource to use with your class. You could also ask them to download it themselves before coming to class. If your group members feel comfortable, it would be fun to take turns reading one of their answers aloud. I would also suggest the couples reading or showing their answers to their partners.

Chapter Ten

This chapter is another one that can be very private for participants. I would recommend letting the group members do it on their own, with an introduction at the beginning. They may not feel comfortable sharing these answers, even with their spouse.

Chapter Eleven

This next chapter is a healing exercise. I only recommend that it be done when someone is no longer triggered by talking about their divorce or bereavement. If anyone does not feel ready, I would suggest that they skip this exercise, and perhaps bring a book or otherwise occupy themselves.

For those who were not divorced or bereaved, they could complete it using their last serious relationship before they married.

This is one exercise that can be very healing for participants to share with their partner, or with another group member if they feel comfortable. The whole point is to help people learn to tell and accept their story without it becoming emotional every time they tell it.

If you find you are short on time, you could even ask the group members to write their answers out the week before. Another way to save on time is to do the "speak your story" version.

Chapter Twelve

This chapter has a lot of information at the beginning. Depending on your time constraints, you may wish to have participants read the beginning part on their own and then go over the first page of questions together. This is a fun exercise to do together as a class because the group would get to hear about these very positive, inspirational couples. After they have finished talking about the older couples that they know, have them finish the last page of questions on their own.

Chapter Thirteen

This chapter is long with four different exercises in it. That is why I have suggested spending one whole class on this chapter. Work your way through the exercises and have fun with them. Anything you don't get done in class, you can suggest the couples try at home. If anyone came without their partner, they would need to do the first two exercises at home with their partner.

The first exercise is just a set of questions to ask each other as a couple. Take turns asking the questions, so person one would ask all the even questions and person two would ask all the odd questions. When the other person is talking, they are not supposed to interrupt or comment. They must be accepting of what their partner is saying, without acting critical or sarcastic. After the person is done talking, they are allowed to ask a clarifying question.

Set a time limit for the first exercise and call when you are done. Even if someone is not quite done, that's okay. It is better to do the second exercise all together. The second exercise is where all the couples will take two minutes and look at one another. After you are done, ask for feedback on how it felt and then watch the suggested video (if you have Internet access.)

Here is link to the video, titled *Couples Stare at Each Other for 4 Minutes Straight | Glamour:*

https://www.youtube.com/watch?v=ONYlKmdylXg

I would suggest that the next two exercises can be done together as couples. If you have people without their spouse, just have them do the exercises on their own.

Chapter Fourteen

This chapter is pretty straightforward. Just work your way through it. Read aloud (you or other members) and have participants fill their answers in as you go. Encourage students to be as honest as possible, so they can grow.

Chapter Fifteen

This chapter has two parts. I would suggest reading out loud together and filling in answers as you go. After the group has done the "Reasons We Argue Questions," have the couples compare the "spouse answers" to see how accurate they are.

For the second exercise, go over the instructions and then let them work on it on their own. Have couples share their answers with one another after they are done.

Chapter Sixteen

This is the longest chapter in the book, and that is why I recommend spending a whole session on this chapter. There is a lot of information here, but it can also be a lot of fun discovering differences and similarities between couples. If you have couples in your session, they each complete their section and then compare whether they are the same or different in each category. If you have people in the group by themselves, have them fill out what they *think* their spouse is, based on observation.

I would suggest reading through each section as a group, giving each couple plenty of time to compare their answers and discuss their similarities/differences and how these similarities and differences can be seen as strengths.

If you have time, you could also get people to share some of their answers with the group as a whole. This could be assuring to hear how other couples manage their differences.

If you run out of time, ask the couples to finish up at home, or you could even finish the exercises up the following week, which is a bit of a shorter week.

Note: This test is based on the Myers-Briggs model and some respondents may already know their type. Even if they already know their type, encourage them to try the quiz. It is fun for couples to compare their answers.

Chapter Seventeen

Please note that chapters 17 and 18 are for those with children at home. If this does apply to certain members of the group, they can come and support other group members or choose to stay home this week.

Chapter 17 is quite short. The members fill in what they think the traditions in their family are, and then ask the children for what they think the traditions are. If you are done with chapters 17 and 18 early, you could either catch up on other chapters or have an open-ended discussion about stepfamily issues. Ask for questions they have and then open the floor to anyone giving their feedback and help.

Chapter Eighteen

This chapter is specifically for stepparents. For the individuals who are not stepparents but their partners are, I would encourage them to listen to understand the concepts, too. The more they understand the stepparent-stepchild dynamic, the better they will be able to offer support.

Please see notes from chapter 17 for the suggestion of what to do if you have extra time after completing chapters 17 & 18.

Chapter Nineteen

Chapters 19-22 are all quite short and that is why I suggest teaching them all in one session. Chapter 19 is very short. You could add in time by having a discussion about things that people are passionate about, and whether or not they are still doing the things they love.

Chapter Twenty

Chapter 20 is very short, too. This chapter is about getting in touch with people that you have cut yourself off from. This chapter may not apply to everyone, so don't spend too much time on it. Simply read through it with the class, explain the idea. You could have a discussion about the reasons that some people may cut themselves off from others when their family problems are overwhelming.

Chapter Twenty-One

This chapter is about counselling or other outside help. I would recommend having everyone take the quiz, even if they think they don't need any other outside help.

Go over the different types of outside help. Add in local resources if you know of some that apply to your area.

Chapter Twenty-Two

This last chapter is very short. Instruct the participants to go back to the Introduction and see what their top three goals were. Encourage them to reflect on what how they have grown in these three areas. Take time to celebrate their accomplishments in finishing the course! You may wish to have a little party or bring in some special food for the end of the course.

Made in United States
Orlando, FL
15 August 2023

36083363R00093